Contents

About the author

Dr Jon Glasby is a lecturer at the University of Birmingham's Health Services Management Centre. His research and publication interests include community care services for older people, the health and social care divide, intermediate care and hospital admissions/discharge.

Author's note

Hospital discharge is a complex and constantly changing area of policy and practice. As a result, many of the individual policies set out in this book are likely to evolve over time. At the time of writing, moreover, we are also expecting new government guidance promised in November 2002. Despite this, many of the underlying themes and issues remain the same, and I hope that this book is a useful introduction to the complexities of hospital discharge irrespective of the exact nature of the policy context.

Acknowledgements

The author is grateful to the many individuals and agencies who have contributed to this book. In particular, he wishes to thank colleagues at the University of Birmingham's Health Services Management Centre, Melanie Henwood, Jo Campling and Radcliffe Medical Press for all their help and support.

List of abbreviations

ADSS	Association of Directors of Social Services
BGS	British Geriatrics Society
DHSSPS	Department of Health, Social Services and Public Safety
DSS/DHSS	Department of Social Security/Health and Social Security
ESAT	Emergency Services Action Team
FHSA	Family Health Services Authority
GP	general practitioner
HIA	Home Improvement Agency
HMSO/TSO	Her Majesty's Stationery Office/The Stationery Office
HOPe	Health and Older People
ISD Scotland	Information and Statistics Division
MRSA	methicillin-resistant *Staphylococcus aureus*
NHS	National Health Service
NI	National Insurance
NISW	National Institute for Social Work
OT	occupational therapy/therapist
PAT	Partnership Assessment Tool
PCG	primary care group
PCT	primary care trust
RCN	Royal College of Nursing
RHA	Regional Health Authority
SPAIN	Social Policy Ageing Information Network
SSD	Social Services Department
SSI	Social Services Inspectorate
STG	Special Transitional Grant
SWSG	Scottish Office Social Work Services Group

CHAPTER 1

Introduction

When Jane (aged 74) was admitted to hospital with chest pains, she was also experiencing bouts of confusion and found that her mobility was rapidly declining. Whilst in hospital, her pains subsided, but no one investigated her other complaints. The ward had a high turnover of patients and wished to discharge Jane back home as soon as possible. Jane's social worker disagreed, saying that Jane did not seem to be medically fit for discharge and that she had unmet health needs which should be explored. Nursing staff replied that they were a surgical ward and did not 'do' confusion or reduced mobility. Having reached something of a stalemate, the ward discharged Jane on a Friday afternoon and only informed the social worker after the event, leaving Jane unsupported at home over the weekend.

Poor practice though it may seem, Jane's story is based on real events and illustrates what can happen when health and social services try (and sometimes fail) to co-ordinate their activities. Although inter-agency collaboration is often complex and problematic, it is hospital discharge rather than any other issue which generates the most tension and causes the most difficulties for the service users and workers involved. As this book will demonstrate, hospital discharge represents a fundamental fault line between two very different services, with different values, priorities and funding mechanisms (Henwood and Wistow 1993; Henwood et al. 1997). Where services work well together, hospital discharges usually proceed in a planned and coherent manner, benefiting patients and practitioners alike. When things go wrong, however, relationships can quickly deteriorate and tempers can fray as different agencies seek to pass responsibilities for particular patients to their 'partners' (Glasby and Littlechild 2000a). As the mutual recriminations begin, there are accusations of 'bed blocking', of 'cost shunting' and of failing to fulfil statutory obligations.

In such a situation, partners seeking to work in a multi-disciplinary fashion quickly polarise, retreating into their 'healthcare' or 'social care' identities. Suddenly, the social care practitioner who queries the appropriateness of a discharge becomes 'a typical social worker unconcerned about pressures on the NHS', whereas the ward sister who wishes to discharge a patient deemed medically fit becomes 'a typical nurse who wants rid of difficult patients'. Although one side is convinced that it is right to emphasise patient choice and time for recuperation, the other is equally adamant that a bed must be vacated for someone else who needs it more than the current occupant. If a resolution is not found, senior managers may become involved and a formal complaint may be made, either by the hospital, by a social worker or by patients and their families. In extreme circumstances, the situation may attract media attention, with the local (and even national) press reporting widespread 'bed blocking' and human misery. As patient throughput is reduced, new admissions may be affected and long waits on trolleys or in hospital corridors provide powerful images on television and in newspapers. This is particularly the case during the winter months, when the annual 'winter crisis' hits the headlines (see, for example, Dymond 1998; Owen 1998).

For practitioners, this state of affairs is highly unsatisfactory. Workers often enter the 'caring professions' because they want to feel that they are helping those in need and making a difference to people's lives. When a hospital ward successfully cares for a patient and discharges them to their own home with an appropriate social care package, everyone involved feels satisfied that they have done their job to the best of their ability and achieved a positive outcome. When a discharge is disputed and becomes problematic, however, it can cause considerable frustration, stress and resentment (often focused on whomever it is that is seen to be holding up the discharge):

> I didn't become a nurse so that social services could block my bed.

> I didn't become a social worker to be at the beck and call of a consultant and care for people who should be in hospital.

For service users and patients, a difficult hospital discharge can be a disruptive and traumatic event. If discharged too soon, the patient can feel unsupported, overwhelmed and unable to cope at home. An already precarious medical condition may then deteriorate, prompting the need for further medical attention or even readmission to hospital. Ultimately, people who do not receive the attention they require can even die, and practitioners involved in health and social care should always be mindful of the profound impact that their actions may have on the lives of the people with whom they work. If a discharge is delayed, the patient remains in hospital longer than is necessary and may suffer as a result. Some people acquire infections, such as methicillin-resistant *Staphylococcus aureus* (MRSA), or find their independence undermined by the hospital regime. Others may be anxious to return home and become depressed due to their enforced inactivity (*see* Chapter 2).

Whether a discharge is too soon or too late, disputes between health and social services can be especially damaging for the individual's self-esteem. Whilst different workers debate what should happen to a patient, they often fail to appreciate the effect that 'being argued over' can have for many people (in particular frail, older people who may already feel as if they are a 'burden' on their families and on scarce public resources). These feelings can also be reinforced by media images of a 'winter crisis' and 'blocked beds', which portray older people in a negative light and may sometimes be internalised by the older people themselves. Certainly, this was a finding in one study in Birmingham, where only two out of 52 older people admitted to hospital as emergency patients dialled '999'. In some cases, this reluctance to seek help was due to a desire not to be a burden and to a belief that someone else would need the hospital bed more than them (Littlechild and Glasby 2000, 2001).

Against this background, policy-makers and local health and social care organisations have adopted a range of initiatives in order to facilitate joint working and improve the quality of hospital discharges. After all, delayed or unco-ordinated discharges not only lead to poor care, but can also have major financial and administrative implications. This can take a number of forms: beds being 'blocked' by people who are medically fit to leave hospital, the costs associated with 'revolving door' readmission of people discharged prematurely, management time taken up with formal complaints and so on. For a range of reasons, therefore, hospital discharge has often been the subject of central policies and local activity. While considerable progress has sometimes been made, however, ensuring appropriate and timely hospital discharges has proved to be a remarkably difficult and intractable problem. Although practice has undoubtedly improved, anecdotal evidence and research findings both suggest that more can and should be done to ensure that patients experience a continuity of care as they move from hospital to the community.

The structure of the book

Although hospital discharge has attracted considerable attention from policy-makers, practitioners and researchers alike, it lacks a comprehensive introductory text which provides an overview of the policy framework, practice issues and research findings. To date, the growing body of literature has tended to fall into one of four categories.

- *Research studies*, which explore the discharge process and methods of improving practice (*see*, for example, Henwood and Wistow 1993; Neill and Williams 1992).
- *Policy documents*, which lay down the responsibilities of health and social care agencies and emphasise the need for closer joint working (*see*, for example, Department of Health 1989b, 1995, 1997c, 2001g).
- *Journalistic accounts* of 'blocked beds' and 'winter crises' (*see*, for example, *Birmingham Evening Mail* 2001; Marsh 2001b).

- *Unpublished and often internal documents*, which explore hospital discharge in specific locations (*see*, for example, Heartlands Hospital Trust/ Birmingham Social Services Department, n.d.). This so-called 'grey' literature may often contain sensitive information and can be unavailable to the general public.

Synthesising such sources, this book begins with an overview of the policy framework, describing the reforms associated with the NHS and Community Care Act 1990 and with the New Labour government which came into power in 1997 (Chapters 2 and 3). Next, Chapters 4 and 5 review a number of key research studies, highlighting the problematic nature of hospital discharge and the consistency of research findings in this area over a period of more than 30 years. After this, Chapters 6 and 7 consider possible ways forward, critiquing current policy initiatives and suggesting alternatives for the future. Lastly, two appendices explore some of the methodological issues associated with measuring delayed hospital discharges (Appendix A) and highlight some of the key milestones associated with intermediate care (Appendix B), a key New Labour policy reviewed earlier in the book.

   Throughout, the main focus of attention is on the hospital discharge of older people, since this user group makes considerable use of health and social services and may have complex and multiple needs that straddle the boundaries of several different agencies or services. For the sake of clarity, the book is also based on services in England, since the health and social care system differs to a greater or lesser extent in other parts of the UK. Despite this, the issues highlighted are likely to be just as relevant for children and younger adults, and references are made wherever possible to the needs and experiences of other user groups and to the experience of Wales, Scotland and Northern Ireland (*see* concluding section of Chapter 5, in particular).

   At various stages in this book, current health and social care policies are evaluated against a framework based on individual, organisational and structural barriers to improved hospital discharge practice and more effective joint working. These three factors may be presented diagrammatically (*see* Figure 1.1) by use of a model already popularised in research into anti-discriminatory practice (Thompson 2001) and adapted in fields such as occupational stress (Glasby 2000b) and organisational change within the voluntary sector (Glasby 2002c). The implications of this model are explored in greater detail in Chapters 5 and 7.

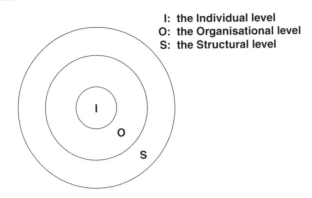

I: the Individual level
O: the Organisational level
S: the Structural level

Figure 1.1   Understanding partnership working in health and social care. (Adapted from Glasby 2000b, 2002c; Thompson 2001.)

A note on terminology

Often, accounts of hospital discharge refer to the problem of 'bed blocking' as a shorthand term for people (often older people) who are felt to be occupying a hospital bed when they no longer need the services provided in an acute setting. Although such phrases are in widespread usage and will be instantly recognised by many readers, this terminology is felt by many to carry a highly pejorative meaning, implying that the older people concerned are themselves to blame for the situation. As this book will demonstrate, however, this is often totally inaccurate, as it is the system itself which causes many such blockages, not individual patients (who often wish to return home as soon as possible). As Victor (1991) explains:

> The whole notion of bed blocking seems to imply that older people enter hospital and then wilfully continue to occupy a bed which, in the views of staff, they no longer require. Older people (or indeed patients of any age) do not become bed blockers of their own intent. Rather where such cases do occur it is because the health and social care system cannot provide the type of care they need. (Victor 1991: p. 123)

As a result, this book tends to adopt more neutral terms, such as 'delayed discharge' wherever possible, referring to 'bed blocking' only where it is absolutely necessary and placing it in inverted commas to highlight the fact that the term is an unsatisfactory one. To its credit, the government has also pledged its commitment to using more appropriate terminology, rejecting the use of the term 'bed blocking' (Department of Health 2002e; House of Commons Health Committee 2002).

CHAPTER 2

The policy framework: 1945–1990

By way of introduction, this chapter seeks to explore the policy context within which hospital discharges take place. A central contention of this book is that the problematic nature of hospital discharge cannot be seen in isolation, but must be viewed as a product of much wider divisions in the welfare state. After reviewing the history of the health and social care divide and the centrality of acute care within the National Health Service (NHS), attention is then focused on the implications of the community care reforms for hospital discharge. Following the passage of the NHS and Community Care Act 1990, social services departments (SSDs) acquired new responsibilities for commissioning services for a range of adult service user groups and collaborative working between health and social care became increasingly significant for swift and effective hospital discharges. Despite this, the reforms also brought increased financial difficulties and tension between health and social care was perhaps inevitable.

The health and social care divide

In many ways, the problematic nature of hospital discharge is closely connected to the structure of welfare services in the UK. Here, there are separate agencies responsible for meeting the health and social care needs of the population, with sharp and well-documented divisions between the two types of organisation (see, for example, Glasby and Littlechild 2000a; Lewis 2001). Although the definition of health and social care is contested and has changed over time, the British welfare state is based on the underlying assumption that it is possible to distinguish between people who are ill or injured (health needs) and people who need lower-level support because of frailty or disability (social needs). Whereas the former will be treated by the NHS, the latter will often fall under the remit of local authority SSDs. Under the current system, moreover, the former are likely to receive their care free of charge while the latter may be called upon to pay for the services they receive (and sometimes to pay considerable sums of money).

In many cases, and at first glance, the distinction between health and social care needs seems to make perfect sense. If a normally fit and healthy adult is injured in a car accident, he or she will be taken to hospital where their injuries will be assessed and treated. Once medically fit to leave hospital, he or she will be discharged home. Should the individual need support with certain activities of daily living whilst recuperating, services may be available from the local SSD to assist with tasks such as housework, shopping or even washing and dressing. Once the individual has fully recovered, he or she will be restored to full fitness and will not require any services at all.

Although this example seems straightforward, it masks a number of complexities. To begin with, it is by no means apparent that assistance with activities of daily living should automatically be classified as a social care need. After all, the need for assistance arises from a medical problem (injuries sustained during a car accident) and the individual may require skilled assistance (if, for example, he or she needs lifting and handling while bathing or getting dressed). Imagine also that the individual concerned is a frail older person with ongoing health and mobility problems, who has slipped and broken a hip. He or she may live in a poorly heated and poorly maintained first-floor flat with a lift that is often out of order. The individual may have little family in the area and be struggling to wash, dress, clean and cook for themselves. As a result, the broken hip is not a one-off crisis in an otherwise healthy person, but the latest in a long line of problems which finally brings the individual into contact with formal services. Against this background, breaking the various issues involved in this scenario down into 'health' and 'social' care needs is complex, controversial and almost entirely arbitrary. Put another way, people do not live their lives according to the categories by which we order our public services, and they often have needs which span the boundaries of traditional service provision.

In the UK, the history of the health and social care divide is difficult to chart, owing to the complexity and fragmentation of the services concerned. In the nineteenth century, the support available for those in need was extremely limited, but tended to take a number of forms (Baggott 1998; Thane 1996).

- *General practitioners* (GPs) were initially private professionals who charged a fee for their services. Gradually, groups of workers unable to afford such fees began to combine together to purchase healthcare through friendly societies.
- *Voluntary hospitals* were established via public subscription or by philanthropy.
- *Other voluntary agencies* were also involved in providing community health services. Working in conjunction with local authorities, they tended to

concentrate on issues such as child welfare, maternity, aftercare, district nursing and disability.

- Initially, too, it was *voluntary bodies*, such as the Charity Organisation Society (Lewis 1995) and the Settlement movement (Glasby 1999, 2000a), which led to the development of the social work profession, pioneering a casework approach to social problems and assessing individuals in need to establish whether or not they were deserving of assistance. In time, both the Charity Organisation Society and the Settlements became involved in setting up social work training courses in conjunction with universities, such as Birmingham, Liverpool and the London School of Economics (*see* Glasby 2001a, for further details).
- *Local authorities* ran municipal hospitals (which developed out of the Poor Law infirmaries of the nineteenth century) as well as specialist hospitals to cater for people suffering from conditions such as tuberculosis, mental ill health and a range of infectious diseases. They also fulfilled an important public health role with powers and responsibilities concerning the water supply, the sewage system, food and hygiene inspection, pollution control, public housing, vaccinations and community health services.

Although health and social service provision had always been fragmented and piecemeal before the second world war, it was the post-war welfare reforms that were to institutionalise the current rigid divisions between health and social care. In the late 1940s, three Acts of Parliament – the National Health Service Act 1946, the National Insurance Act 1946 and the National Assistance Act 1948 – established a new framework for meeting the welfare needs of British citizens that continues to underpin current services in the early twenty-first century. Henceforth:

- *financial assistance* for those on low incomes would be available via the social security system
- *health care* would be provided for those in need of constant nursing or medical attention via the NHS
- local authorities would be responsible for residential care and a range of domiciliary services (including some health-related services, such as health visiting and home nursing) for those in need of constant care and attention.

Under this, and subsequent legislation, healthcare was to be provided free at the point of delivery, while social care could incur charges. Many of the community health functions initially retained by local authorities were subsequently transferred to health authorities under the NHS Act 1973.

During the second half of the twentieth century, a key feature of welfare provision for older people has been the way in which services traditionally seen as falling under the remit of the NHS have gradually been redefined as social care (Hudson 2000; Means 1986; Means and Smith 1998b), thereby exposing service users to often significant charges for services they once thought would be provided free of charge. As a result, residential and nursing homes have begun to cater for service users with much greater health needs than would previously have been admitted, patients are discharged from hospital much more quickly than would once have been the case and hospitals have greatly reduced the number of long-stay beds for people with ongoing health needs. Despite government attempts to encourage greater collaboration between health and social care services (*see below*), considerable financial, administrative and professional divisions make successful inter-agency working just as elusive as it has always been throughout the post-war period (*see* Box 2.1 and Box 2.2. *See also* Glasby and Littlechild 2000a; Lewis 2001; Means and Smith 1998b).

Box 2.1 The health and social care divide

- **Local authority SSDs**
  Democratically elected
  Overseen by the Office of the Deputy Prime Minister
  Subject to means-testing and charges
  Cover specific geographical areas
  Traditional focus on social factors contributing to individual situations
    and on choice/empowerment
  Strong emphasis on social sciences
- **NHS**
  Appointed by central government
  Overseen by Department of Health
  Free at point of delivery
  Boundaries are based on GP registration
  Traditional emphasis on the individual and on medical cure
  Strong emphasis on science

Box 2.2 Barriers to inter-agency collaboration

- *Structural* (fragmentation of service responsibilities across agency boundaries, within and between sectors)
- *Procedural* (differences in planning horizons and cycles; differences in budgetary cycles and procedures; differences in information systems and protocols regarding confidentiality and access)

continued opposite

- *Financial* (differences in funding mechanisms and bases; differences in the stocks and flows of financial resources)
- *Professional* (professional self-interest and autonomy, and inter-professional competition for domains; threats to job security; conflicting views about clients or consumers' interests and roles)
- *Status and legitimacy* (organisational self-interest and autonomy and inter-organisational competition for domains; differences in legitimacy between elected and appointed agencies)

Source: Hudson *et al.* 1997, p. 11

The importance of acute hospital beds

Ever since the foundation of the NHS, healthcare in the UK has been dominated by acute hospital beds. Not only do acute beds consume a significant proportion of NHS resources (Baggott 1998, p. 129), they are also the dominant form of healthcare from the point of view of the general public. When people think of the NHS they think of beds, and any attempt to shift the balance between acute and community services may be interpreted as a threat to hospital beds and generate widespread protest. Recent examples have occurred in areas such as Kent and Kidderminster, where campaigners have mounted high-profile bids to save their local hospitals (*see*, for example, Maloney 2001; Moore 2002; Thorne 2001; Timmins 2001; *see also* Box 2.3).

Box 2.3   The power of protest

In the Wyre Forest, dissatisfaction with the downgrading of Kidderminster Hospital has led to considerable local protest and the election of a series of 'Health Concern' campaigners as local councillors and as the area's Member of Parliament.

'When campaigners fighting to save Kidderminster Hospital swept all before them at the 1999 local elections their critics said it would never last. A year later the good people of Wyre Forest went back to the ballot box and instead of returning to their traditional allegiances the electorate made the Health Concern group the most powerful in the district. The group, which is fighting for a complete return of accident and emergency services at Kidderminster Hospital, now boasts 19 seats on Wyre Forest District Council and is the largest member of the ruling Rainbow Alliance.'

Source: Thorne 2001

continued overleaf

'It used to be perceived wisdom that independent candidates, deprived of the clout of a national political machine, could not win under the British political system … Now in Worcestershire's Wyre Forest, a traditionally Conservative seat turned into a Labour marginal, there is a growing possibility that the underdog may … have his day. Dr Richard Taylor, a 66-year-old retired consultant physician at Kidderminster General Hospital is making all the running in his local campaign. His issue is the local hospital and it is every health planner's and party politician's nightmare. Last September, Kidderminster lost its accident and emergency department and 192 acute beds … Kidderminster … was much-loved. It has just received millions in what is now wasted new investment and its planned down-grading coincided with controversial plans for a privately financed new hospital at Worcester, some 18 miles but often a 40-minute journey away on busy roads. The constituency erupted.'

Source: Timmins 2001

Over time there is considerable evidence to suggest that acute hospital beds are being used inappropriately, either by people admitted to hospital when they could be cared for in alternative settings, or by people who are medically fit to leave but are unable to do so for a number of reasons (*see* Chapters 4 and 5 for more details). According to one estimate, the rate of inappropriate bed use by older people may be approximately 20% of all bed days (McDonagh *et al.* 2000). Put another way, one day in every five that older people spend in hospital is probably unnecessary. Such a situation is problematic for a number of reasons.

- *Hospital beds* are expensive and inappropriate bed use is a waste of scarce public resources. Work undertaken by the Personal Social Services Research Unit suggests that one inpatient day for an older person costs approximately £144 (Netten *et al.* 2001), so there is considerable scope for efficiency savings by reducing the number of beds occupied inappropriately. Thus, a study in inner London found that 74 patients inappropriately located in hospital accrued 7519 inappropriate bed days at a cost of £836 547 (Victor *et al.* 1993a).
- There is a *finite number* of acute hospital beds and sometimes there may not be enough capacity to admit patients who require hospital care. This is particularly the case during the winter months, although evidence suggests that pressure on beds can now occur at any time of the year (Moore 1995; NHS Confederation 1997). An extreme example comes from Birmingham, where patients were treated in ambulances because the accident and emergency department was full and the hospital was

unable to free up beds by discharging patients medically fit to leave because of funding difficulties in the local SSD (Marsh 2001a and 2001c).

- *Hospital* is often an unsuitable environment for people fit for discharge. Unnecessarily long hospital stays can subject patients to the risk of hospital-acquired infections and delayed discharges may lead to depression or a decline in functional independence. Many patients also prefer to be in the comfort of their own homes if at all possible and many find prolonged hospital stays frustrating and/or distressing.

For economic, administrative and humanitarian reasons, therefore, delayed discharges from acute hospital beds are generally perceived to be problematic by policy-makers, practitioners and patients alike.

Hospital discharge and the community care reforms

From 1948 onwards, hospital discharge has been seen as a potential source of tension within both the NHS and social care, with policy-makers and practitioners alike concerned to limit the potential problem of 'blocked beds' and establish which service should be responsible for frail older people (*see* Means and Smith 1998b, for an overview of the development of services for older people since the second world war; *see also* Box 2.4). For example:

- *During the 1930s*, a shortage of hospital beds for older people meant that the 'chronic sick' were discharged to non-hospital beds in order to make room for new admissions.
- *During the second world war*, there were fears that rest centres for those whose homes had been damaged by the war would become blocked by frail older people unable to look after themselves (the so-called 'unbilletables'). The 'chronic sick' were also seen as blocking scarce hospital beds.
- *In the late 1940s and 1950s*, the Boucher Report (1957) emphasised the need for more residential homes to enable the discharge of some 4500 patients currently in hospital but no longer requiring the services provided there. There were also concerns about 'bed blocking' from the British Medical Association (BMA) (1948) and from hospital authorities across the country. There was also a growing awareness of the need for some sort of 'half-way house' or intermediate service between a hospital and a residential home.
- To attempt to clarify the boundary between hospital and residential care, the Ministry of Health issued guidance in *the 1950s and 1960s* (Ministry of Health 1957a, 1957b, 1965). Although seeking to clarify

which type of patient should receive which type of service, the guidance was riddled with ambiguities and probably resulted in considerable local debate over individual cases (Means and Smith 1998b). This has been described by Davies (1979, pp. 16–17) in terms of a 'swap', with hospitals refusing to accept patients from residential care unless the residential home in question first agreed to accept a patient discharged from the hospital.

- Possible solutions were debated at various stages *in the second half of the twentieth century,* including the restoration of hospital services to the local authority, the creation of a single health and social care service or mechanisms to create more co-ordinated planning between health and social care agencies.

Box 2.4 Hospital discharge and the health and social care divide*

Problems raised by chronic sickness are important but have been neglected in most schemes for medical reorganisation. Chronic sick patients are numerous especially in the higher age groups, and their long occupancy of beds holds up a high percentage of the total accommodation.

Source: Samson 1944, p. 52

The scheme [that is, 1940s legislation with regard to the NHS and national assistance] may well fail unless, through the establishment of standing liaison committees, means are found to bring about such close co-ordination of the functions of the various authorities as will ensure the free passage of elderly people, under the expert guidance of the geriatric department, from home to hospital and from hospital to home in accordance with their changing needs.

Source: Anderson Report 1947, p. 12

Some 60% of patients now occupying beds in hospitals for the chronic sick do not need frequent medical attention nor skilled nursing. Only about one-half of admissions are justified on medical grounds; the other half just have nowhere else to go. If there were rest homes for these old people, with simple nursing and general care, there would be an enormous increase in the number of beds available for old and young who really need hospital care. The provision of these rest homes would go far to remedy another of our failures: the old people who are stranded in the no man's land between the regional Hospital Board and the local welfare department – not ill enough for one, not well enough for the other.

Source: Huws Jones 1952, p. 22

continued opposite

There is unfortunately a wide gulf between the aids given by the Regional Hospital Board and those administered by the Local Authority. Hence the needs of the elderly frequently fall between the two bodies – the individual being not sick enough to justify admission to a hospital and yet too disabled or frail for a vacancy in a Home.

Source: Warren 1951, p. 106

Of the patients discharged from the geriatric unit during the period under review, about a third went to hostels or old people's homes: more could have been discharged had the vacancies been available. But the greatest need was for a more sheltered type of hostel for the frail old person, not in need of hospital care yet incapable of climbing flights of stairs ... These perforce had to remain in a hospital bed.

Source: Andrews and Wilson 1953, pp. 785–789

The chronic aged sick are surely the biggest 'headache' confronting the mental health world. It appears that many of them occupy beds that might be more profitably occupied by younger patients who could be cured and returned to activity of some value to the national economy.

Source: Maddison 1954, p. 983

*All extracts quoted from Means and Smith 1998b.

Official guidance

In 1963, the Ministry of Health issued guidance, *Discharge of Patients from Hospital and Arrangements for After-Care* (Ministry of Health 1963), to all hospital authorities, as well as to local authorities and to doctors in general practice. Claiming not to introduce any new principles, but merely to embody principles generally accepted as good practice, the circular emphasised that (Ministry of Health 1963, para. 2–3):

> Adequate and timely after-care arrangements are not only in the interest of certain types of patient but will prevent beds being occupied by patients who no longer need hospital care. Hospital authorities are asked to ensure – and constantly to verify – that each person in the line of communication realizes his responsibility, and to designate, where necessary, officers to perform the functions described in the memorandum.

In particular, the circular suggested that the procedures required for a satisfactory discharge were 'simple and often obvious' (para. 2), but that difficulties could occur due to communication failures. Since particular groups of people – those living alone, older people, disabled people and some maternity patients – may need additional help on leaving hospital, discharge arrangements should fully consider social as well as medical factors (para. 2):

> The full benefit of hospital treatment may well be lost if arrangements for after-care are inadequate. The object is to enable all patients after discharge to feel secure and, as far as possible, to be self-reliant ... It is important that in all cases, ... full account should be taken of social as well as medical considerations when arranging discharge from hospital. The patient's home circumstances – for instance, whether he has relatives or friends who can look after him – are a big factor in determining what after-care he needs.

When a patient is ready to be discharged, the doctor in charge of the case should inform the patient and the GP (perhaps using a sample letter provided in an appendix to the circular). A key role is also played by the ward sister, who ensures that the relevant people have been notified, that transport is provided where necessary and that the patient has sufficient drugs and dressings. Where community services or continued rehabilitation are required, the hospital almoner becomes involved and may refer the case to the local authority. This should happen at least 48 hours before discharge so that suitable arrangements may be made. To facilitate the discharge process, the circular also suggests that it is useful for the local authority to appoint one or more officers to be specifically responsible for mobilizing appropriate services (including voluntary sector services) after discharge from hospital. Throughout, the patient and their relatives should be kept informed about what is happening (para. 9–10):

> The relative (if any) responsible for the patient is told the intended date of discharge by telephone, by written notice, or on the next visit if time allows. The ward sister ensures that the relative understands what he has to do and that he is aware of any help that is being arranged or can be got from the local authority or voluntary services. She [the ward sister] discusses with him [the relative] arrangements for transport of the patient ..., tells him of any drugs or dressings the patient is taking with him ..., and of any arrangements to be made for the patient to be seen by his general practitioner. The patient is bound to be anxious about his discharge, and keeping him fully informed will allay unnecessary anxieties. The Minister commends the practice of some hospital authorities in issuing a booklet summarising what the patient should know about hospital procedure and facilities available on discharge, what he himself should do and to whom he should turn in case of difficulty. Some local authorities also help hospitals in this by supplying a booklet giving details of the community services.

Following the 1963 circular, there was no more official guidance on hospital discharge until 1989 – 26 years later. Even then, the 1989 circular HC(89)5/LAC(89)7 was issued not as a pro-active move by government to update policy, but as a response to criticism from the House of Commons Select Committee on the Parliamentary Commissioner for Administration (*see* Box 2.5).

Box 2.5   Background to the 1989 hospital discharge guidance

Those concerned with the quality of clinical care recognise the importance of good discharge arrangements. However the Select Committee
on the Parliamentary Commissioner for Administration has criticised
the lack of up to date guidance on discharge arrangements and made
it clear that they attached high priority to its issue and to action by
authorities to implement the necessary procedures. Points which
were emphasised by the Committee included the need

- to provide families with the necessary information and reassurance about the care of the patient after discharge
- to check on day of departure that the patient was fit to leave hospital
- to inform the patient's general practitioner/community nursing
  services/social services of the patient's potential needs in time for
  them to be met
- to secure therapy assessment prior to discharge to ensure facilities in
  the home were appropriate to the needs of the patient concerned.
  Source: Department of Health 1989b

Issued to all local authorities, health authorities and family practitioner
committees, the 1989 circular emphasised 'the importance of ensuring
that, before patients are discharged from hospital, proper arrangements
are made for their return home and for any continuing care which may be
necessary'. To this end, District and Special Health Authorities were to
ensure that all wards/departments have up-to-date discharge procedures
agreed with all those involved in the discharge process, issue the procedures
to all concerned, monitor and amend their procedures as appropriate and
report to the Regional Health Authority on any action taken. Throughout
the circular, a number of central themes are immediately apparent:

- planning for discharge should begin at an early stage (before or as soon
  as possible after admission)
- discharge planning and arrangements should include primary and
  social care where appropriate
- the patient and his or her family must be at the centre of the planning
  process
- no one should be discharged without the authority of the doctor responsible
  for the patient concerned
- this doctor should not allow patients to be discharged until satisfied that
  everything reasonably practicable has been done to organise the care
  which the patient will need in the community

- one member of staff caring for the patient should take responsibility for checking that all necessary action has been taken prior to discharge, using a checklist of what needs to be done
- patients must receive written information about issues such as medication, diet and symptoms to watch for
- local authorities have a key role to play in arranging services for the minority of patients who need ongoing support after discharge and should assess such patients at an early stage prior to discharge
- in some situations, local authority housing departments will need to be involved in discharge planning.

Attached to the guidance was a booklet providing further details of the areas which hospital discharge procedures should cover. Although the full contents are summarised later in this book (*see* Table 3.1 in Chapter 3), the booklet gave general guidance on which workers might be responsible for particular areas of the discharge process. This included individual sections on the tasks to be completed by the consultant or medical team, the ward sister or nursing team, paramedical services, maternity services, social services, primary care, community nursing services and ambulance services. A brief appendix also provided details of publications which set out good practice for patients from particular specialties. Overall, key themes to emerge from the booklet include the importance of defining the responsibilities of all staff involved in hospital discharge, the need for good communication, the importance of liaising with social services and housing at an early stage and the need to make sure that any support required is in place before the patient is discharged.

Although the 1989 circular was much more detailed than what had gone before, there were three key limitations. First, evidence suggests that the circular was not properly implemented and that many problems still persist, many years after the circular was issued (*see* Chapters 4 and 5). Second, the onus for improving hospital discharge practice fell very much on individual practitioners and on local health and social care agencies, with very little apparent recognition of wider barriers to joint working (*see* Chapter 7 for a further discussion). Lastly (and with hindsight), the true significance of the 1989 guidance may well lie in the insight it provides into the formation of policy in Whitehall. The circular was issued in 1989 at the same time as the government was considering a fundamental reform of health and particularly social care (*see below*). Although the reforms were to have profound implications for hospital discharge, the circular made no reference whatsoever to the imminent NHS and Community Care Act 1990. To the cynic, this might seem to be evidence of a lack of planning at the heart of central government and a failure on the part of policy-makers to produce a coherent and co-ordinated vision for the way forward.

Developments in the 1980s

Although discharging people from hospital has long been a controversial and complex task, discharge has acquired increasing significance since the NHS and Community Care Act 1990. Before the full implementation of the Act in 1993, there was a degree of flexibility in the system, with hospital patients able to be discharged directly into residential or nursing homes with funding from the Department of Health and Social Security (DHSS – later the Department of Social Security or DSS). This had been made possible by changes in Supplementary Benefit (now Income Support) regulations in the early 1980s, with the DHSS beginning to make 'board and lodgings' payments for people in non-local authority homes (*see* Audit Commission 1986; Bradshaw 1988; Laing 1993; Tinker 1997). This was initially a discretionary process set up in response to financial difficulties in local authorities and amongst independent residential or nursing homes following the oil crisis and the subsequent economic dislocations of the late 1970s. To begin with, the DHSS began to make payments for the care of those residents 'unable to afford their own fees and for whom local authorities were unwilling to foot the bill' (Laing 1993, p. 25). This practice was later formalised, leading to a massive increase in the number of independent sector homes and the number of residents being supported by the DHSS. As a result, social security expenditure on Income Support for people in independent sector residential and nursing homes in Britain rose from £10 million in 1979 to £2575 million in 1993, with the number of individual recipients increasing from 11 000 to a peak of 281 000 over the same period (quoted in Tinker 1997, p. 157).

Of course, looking back over a number of years it is difficult to be certain how widespread the practice of discharging patients directly into residential or nursing care might have been or how appropriate this type of service may have been for the people concerned. Whatever the gaps in our current knowledge, however, three key issues are immediately apparent.

1 The number of admissions to private residential or nursing homes increased dramatically following the changes in social security policy described above. By the early 1990s, hundreds of thousands of people were receiving financial contributions to the cost of their care, with no objective assessment of their need for the services they were using.
2 Many of those admitted to independent sector homes were less dependent than people in local authority homes (for which Supplementary Benefit was unavailable). This has been demonstrated by a host of research studies (*see*, for example, Bebbington and Tong 1986), and it is only relatively recently that levels of dependency have begun to even out between homes in the public and independent sectors.

3 Hospital staff may sometimes overestimate the level and duration of support which older patients require, prematurely 'writing them off' as suitable only for residential or nursing care (*see*, for example, Littlechild *et al*. 1995).

Viewed from this angle, it seems difficult to escape the conclusion that a substantial number of people in the 1980s may have been admitted to residential and nursing care, not because they needed the support provided by these services, but because of the relatively easy availability of public funds. Although we can probably never be certain, it also seems likely that a number of older hospital patients were prematurely admitted to institutional forms of care by hospital staff, not necessarily because they needed 24-hour care, but because they simply did not need to be in hospital and because the availability of DHSS funding provided something of a safety valve in the system.

The community care reforms

By the late 1980s, this state of affairs was perceived to be unsatisfactory for a variety of reasons:

• public expenditure on residential or nursing care was increasing dramatically, seemingly spiralling out of control
• this was not only expensive, but also diverted resources towards institutional forms of care and away from community services. For the Audit Commission (1986, pp. 43–48), the availability of Supplementary Benefit for residential or nursing care was a 'perverse' incentive that hindered the development of community-based forms of support. For Sir Roy Griffiths (1988, p. 9), architect of the community care reforms, 'the separate funding of residential and nursing home care through social security, with no assessment of need, is a particularly pernicious split in responsibilities, and a fundamental obstacle to the creation of a comprehensive local approach to community care'.
• DHSS support was available on the basis of income alone, with those without sufficient funds to pay for their own care receiving public support irrespective of their health status, their level of disability or frailty or their 'need' for residential or nursing care. For Griffiths (1988, p. v), this could easily lead to a situation where 'the ready availability of social security makes it easy to provide residential accommodation for an individual regardless of whether it is in his best interest'.

As a result, two of the key aims of the NHS and Community Care Act 1990 (*see* Box 2.6) were 'to make proper assessment of need ... the cornerstone of high quality care' and 'to secure better value for taxpayers' money by introducing a new funding structure for social care' (Department of Health 1989a, p. 5). The resultant legislative and policy changes were complex, and have been described in detail elsewhere (*see*, for example, Means and Smith 1998a; Victor 1997). However, after the full implementation of the Act in 1993, local authorities were to take the lead in assessing individuals' needs, designing care packages and securing their delivery within available resources. This was to include those entering residential and nursing care, who would now need to be assessed by a social worker before admission and whose care would now be funded by a local authority SSD with money transferred from the DHSS via a new Special Transitional Grant (STG). Perhaps unsurprisingly, the latter involved complex calculations, based in part on the social security payments that would have been made to people in residential and nursing care had the pre-1993 system continued (*see* Glasby and Glasby 1999, 2002 for a more detailed discussion of social work and local government finance).

Box 2.6   The NHS and Community Care Act 1990

The Government believes that for most people community care offers the best form of care available – certainly with better quality and choice than they might have expected in the past. The changes outlined in this White Paper are intended to:

- enable people to live as normal a life as possible in their own homes or in a homely environment in the community;
- provide the right amount of care and support to help people achieve maximum possible independence and, by acquiring or reacquiring basic living skills, help them achieve their full potential;
- give people a greater individual say in how they live their lives and the services they need to help them do so.

Source: Department of Health 1989a, p. 4

While many government documents emphasised the humanitarian and benevolent nature of the community care reforms (*see*, for example, Box 2.6 above), there is little doubt that the 1990 Act was also a response to pressing financial issues. Public expenditure on residential or nursing care was rising rapidly with no assessment of need (other than financial) and no means of halting the ongoing increases. Since local authorities have finite budgets and have to balance a host of competing demands, the decision to transfer responsibility for funding residential or nursing care to SSDs meant that the task of restricting the rapidly increasing social security bill would fall to local authorities. When local authority SSDs complain of a lack of funds, therefore, (*see*, for example, Community Care 1998) it is worth remembering that such financial difficulties are an almost inevitable consequence of the 1990 community care reforms. Put another way, community care may be seen as a deliberate attempt by government to transfer financial pressures from a central department to local government in the hope that the latter would be able to constrain the rise in public expenditure. As a result, financial tensions were always going to develop once the Act came into force.

Coupled with the financial pressures on which the 1990 Act was founded were technical difficulties in the STG formula used to redirect resources from the DSS to local authority SSDs. This is a complicated issue, but has been explained in more detail in a recent handbook on local government finance (*see* Box 2.7).

Box 2.7 The limits of STG

1 Many commentators feel that the STG was insufficient to enable local authorities to meet their responsibilities for funding community care. Part of the STG was based on how much the DSS previously spent on Income Support claimants in institutional care (the DSS transfer element). Calculating this was complicated and the final estimates were strongly contested by local authority associations, who felt that the information used to make these calculations was inadequate. The Association of Metropolitan Authorities later claimed that the STG in its first year fell short of the true cost of the reforms by some £289 million and predicted a further shortfall of £800 million by 1997 …

2 The formula for calculating the STG initially took considerable note of previous DSS spending on Income Support claimants in residential care. This created a disincentive for councils to transfer resources from residential to domiciliary care, one of the key aims of the community care reforms. This anomaly was resolved in 1994 when the formula for calculating the STG was changed.

3 The cost of community care was a major political and financial issue on the eve of the 1990 reforms. Transferring resources for resolving this issue to local authorities was not in itself a solution and some degree of financial difficulty and controversy was inevitable. In many ways, the problems involved in funding institutional care still remain …

4 The way in which the STG was phased out in 1997–1998 was handled in a less than transparent way, with the government keen to emphasise the increased budgets which it had granted to local authorities. In the process, it neglected to mention that much of this 'increase' was actually the result of incorporating the old STG

continued opposite

---

into mainstream funding and did not represent 'new' revenue in any way. This created considerable confusion at a local level, where members of the public were understandably unable to reconcile the government's claim to have increased local authority budgets with their councils' current financial difficulties.

Source: Glasby and Glasby 1999, pp. 22–23

From this discussion of some of the main features of the community care reforms, we can see that changes in the early 1990s were to have two key implications for hospital discharge.

1 Hospitals would no longer be able to discharge patients to residential or nursing care with funding from the DSS. Instead, they would have to rely upon their local authority SSD carrying out an assessment of individual patients' needs and securing appropriate services.
2 For a variety of reasons, the local authorities concerned were likely to face significant financial pressures as the new system bedded down.

With hindsight, these two issues may account for many of the difficulties and tensions highlighted in Chapters 4 and 5.

Summary

Hospital discharge represents a key dividing line between health and social care, and there are a range of structural barriers to closer joint working. Concerns about services for older people and about 'bed blocking' have been voiced over and over again since the mid-twentieth century, and there are important humanitarian, economic and administrative reasons for ensuring that hospital beds and scarce public resources are used as appropriately as possible.

Although the health and social care divide is a longstanding issue, hospital discharge has acquired even greater prominence following the community care reforms of the early 1990s. From 1993 onwards, hospitals and SSDs were going to have to work much more closely together in order to ensure effective and timely hospital discharges, yet would have to do so in a climate characterised by the imperative to curtail rapidly increasing public expenditure on residential and nursing care.

CHAPTER 3

The policy framework: the 1990s and beyond

Following the initial policy overview provided in Chapter 2, this chapter considers developments in the 1990s and the early twenty-first century. This includes the approaches adopted by a series of Conservative administrations, as well as by the New Labour government elected in May 1997. Although changes in ethos and emphasis are apparent, the underlying theme is one of continuity, with central government policy by and large failing to engage with the complexity of hospital discharge and the health and social care divide.

Despite the importance of community care for hospital discharge, it is surprising that these issues did not attract more attention during the debates surrounding the Community Care Act. Thus, there were no references whatsoever to hospital discharge in the Act itself, and an attempted amendment that would have made an assessment of people leaving hospital mandatory was not successful (Mandelstam 1999, p. 375). Whilst policy and practice guidance did make brief references to the issue of discharge and recognised that some change was likely (Department of Health 1990, p. 31; Department of Health/SSI/SWSG 1991, pp. 92–93), the relevant passages were very cursory and mainly served to reiterate the contents of the 1989 circular (*see* Box 3.1 for examples). A classic example is provided by the White Paper, *Caring for People*, which states that 'health authorities will … need to work closely with social services authorities to arrange care for elderly people inappropriately placed in hospital' (Department of Health 1989a, p. 49), without clarifying what exactly 'working closely together' should entail or how this should be achieved.

Box 3.1   Policy and practice guidance

The decision to admit to, or to discharge from, hospital is taken primarily on medical grounds but it also has to take account of social and other factors. Wherever these factors come into play, there should be close consultation between health authorities and SSDs … Local

continued overleaf

> assessment arrangements for services required by a patient following discharge from hospital will need to be reviewed in the light of the new responsibilities local authorities will have. As explained in existing circulars on hospital discharge ... health authorities, in conjunction with local authorities, are responsible for designating staff to develop, implement and monitor individual discharge plans.
>
> *Source*: Department of Health 1990, p. 31
>
> The transfer of funding responsibility to local authorities in April 1993 will mean that hospital discharge arrangements have to be revised. In England, the responsibility of health authorities, in conjunction with local authorities, to designate specific staff to develop, implement and monitor individual discharge plans, as set out in the existing circulars on hospital discharge, is unchanged.
>
> *Source*: Department of Health/SSI/SWSG 1991, pp. 92–93

Perhaps in recognition of the relative neglect of hospital discharge, there was a flurry of official activity during 1991–1992, shortly before the Act was to be fully implemented in April 1993. In 1991, the Patient's Charter reiterated the emphasis of the 1989 circular on consulting users and carers and making arrangements for care needs before discharge takes place (Department of Health 1991, p. 15):

> Before you are discharged from hospital a decision should be made about any continuing health and social care needs you may have. Your hospital will agree arrangements for meeting these needs with agencies such as community nursing services and local authority social services departments before you are discharged. You and, with your agreement, your carers will be consulted and informed at all stages.

In March 1992, the Deputy Chief Executive of the NHS Management Executive and the Chief Inspector of the Social Services Inspectorate (SSI) wrote to Directors of Social Services, Regional General Managers, District General Managers, FHSA General Managers and Chief Executives of NHS Trusts to set out expectations regarding the work required over the next 12 months in order to secure a 'smooth transition' to the new arrangements for community care (Department of Health 1992a, p. 1). Often referred to as the first Foster–Laming letter (after the names of the two authors), the document identified eight 'key tasks' on which local authorities, working closely with other agencies (including health authorities) would need to concentrate in 1992–1993 (*see* Box 3.2). Of these, one of the tasks was to ensure 'the robustness and mutual acceptability of discharge arrangements', jointly reviewing discharge policies to ensure that they 'take full account of the new requirement for [local authorities] to introduce needs based assessment and that there is always a clear understanding of the services to be made available to the individual following discharge' (Department of Health 1992a, p. 2 and Annex B).

Box 3.2   The 'eight key tasks'

- Agreeing the basis for required assessment systems for individuals
- Clarifying and agreeing arrangements for continuing care for new clients in residential and nursing homes including arrangements for respite care
- **Ensuring the robustness and mutual acceptability of discharge arrangements**
- Clarifying roles of GPs and primary health care teams
- Ensuring that adequate purchasing and charging arrangements are in place in respect of individuals who will be receiving residential or nursing home care
- Ensuring that financial and other management systems can meet the new demands likely after 1 April 1993
- Ensuring that staff are suitably trained, wherever appropriate on a joint basis
- Informing the public of the arrangements made by the authority for assessment and the provision of care
  Source: Department of Health 1992a, p. 2 [emphasis added]

In September 1992, the second Foster–Laming letter reiterated the importance of the eight key tasks and the need for further action in a number of key areas (Department of Health 1992b). In particular, the letter called for local and health authorities to reach agreements by 31 December 1992 on their respective responsibilities for placing people in nursing homes, the numbers of people likely to be involved and how hospital discharge arrangements would be integrated with assessment arrangements (*see* Box 3.3). In October 1992 it was announced that evidence of these December 31st Agreements (as they became known) would have to be provided as a condition of the payment of the Special Transitional Grant designed to finance the transfer of funding responsibilities from the DSS to local authorities (Department of Health 1992c, 1992d). Also in 1992 came the creation of a Community Care Support Force to disseminate good practice on the eight key tasks and support the implementation of the community care reforms.

Box 3.3   December 31st Agreements

Close co-operation between health and social services authorities in addressing the eight key tasks will be essential. Co-operation needs to go beyond the process of joint planning to include detailed

continued overleaf

agreements on the responsibilities and contributions (in staff and resource terms) of each agency and joint commitment to implementation. While previous rounds of monitoring show that joint working is being strengthened, it is clear that further progress needs to be made. We consider it essential that all authorities reach agreements by 31 December on:

- agreed strategies governing health and local authority responsibilities for placing people in nursing homes, and the numbers likely to be involved during 1993–94;
- how hospital discharge arrangements will be integrated with assessment arrangements.

Source: Department of Health 1992b, p. 2

This letter sets out the Government's intentions for the funding arrangements for local authorities' new responsibilities [for community care] … Authorities' attention is drawn in particular to paragraphs 22 to 29 of the [attached] memorandum. Ministers firmly intend to link payment of the special transitional [grant] to the receipt of evidence by **31 December 1992** that authorities have reached the agreements with District Health Authorities set out in paragraph 4 of the Foster/Laming letter of 25 September. These agreements are on:

- agreed strategies governing health and local authority responsibilities for placing people in nursing homes, and the numbers likely to be involved during 1993–94
- how hospital discharge arrangements will be integrated with assessment arrangements.

Source: Department of Health 1992c [emphasis in the original]

Following the introduction of the community care reforms, there was further activity in the mid-1990s to improve hospital discharge practices after ongoing evidence of considerable difficulties (*see* Chapters 4 and 5). In 1994, the Department of Health published the *Hospital Discharge Workbook* to develop a framework for good practice that addressed both quality and efficiency issues, focused on outcomes for service users and the overall service, provided practical help and recognised the range of stakeholders concerned with hospital discharge (Henwood 1994). Produced by a working group which combined considerable research and practical experience (*see* Box 3.4), the workbook was edited by Melanie Henwood, a leading researcher on hospital discharge whose work is frequently cited throughout this book (*see* Chapters 4 and 5 for further details).

Box 3.4   The *Hospital Discharge Workbook* working group members

- Brian Ferguson, Deputy Director, Health Economics Consortium, University of York
- Melanie Henwood, Visiting Fellow, Nuffield Institute for Health, Community Care Division
- Dr Tim Hill, GP, Shrewsbury
- Paul Jenkins, Community Care Unit, NHS Executive Headquarters
- Jacqueline Johnston, Community Care Unit, NHS Executive Headquarters
- Nigel Jones, Community Care Unit, NHS Executive Headquarters (then with the Community Care Division, Nuffield Institute for Health)
- Jenny McMullan, Unit Manager, Health and Community Services, Kirklees Social Services
- Dr Jackie Morris, Senior Medical Officer, Department of Health, and Consultant in Medicine of Old Age
- Chris Norris, Line-up Video Marketing Ltd
- Wendy Pearson, General Manager, Scunthorpe General Hospital
- Edna Robinson, Director of Community Care, Manchester DHAs Purchasing Consortium
- Diana Sanderson, Health Economics Consortium, University of York
- Christabel Shawcross, Inspector, Social Services Inspectorate
- Paul Thacker, Team Leader, CNS Liaison, West Suffolk Hospital
- Stuart Turnock, Project Manager, Audit Commission
- Judi Wellden, Community Development Manager, North Tyneside Health Authority
- Liz Wolstenholme, Head of Community Care Unit, NHS Executive Headquarters

Source: Henwood 1994, p. 17

To maximise its potential contribution, the workbook was designed to be used as a self-audit tool, with key questions for relevant stakeholders to address, examples of innovative practice, a checklist for managers and practitioners, and a series of performance indicators. Beginning with pre-admission, the document follows the discharge process through admission, assessment, the hospital stay, discharge and monitoring or evaluation. Throughout, the key issues are broken down for the various stakeholders with organisational responsibility for discharge: senior strategic managers, hospital and social services managers, community-based health and social services and hospital-based practitioners. Crucially, the workbook seeks to emphasise the essential compatibility of successful outcomes for users and carers, on the one hand, and resource effectiveness, on the other. Good practice, in other words, is not an optional luxury that can only occur at the expense of, and with considerable disruption to, health and social services: it is resource-efficient (Henwood 1994, p. 4).

> The central focus of the workbook is with the outcomes of hospital discharge, both for the individual service user, and in terms of resource effectiveness. Too often these objectives are perceived as incompatible. In fact, the workbook offers a process through which both sets of objectives can be pursued in parallel. Outcomes which are good for individuals are also a good use of resources; and the best use of resources should produce good individual outcomes.

A second key feature of the workbook was its explicit recognition that health and social services are interdependent, and that action in one area will inevitably have consequences for other agencies. As a result, the workbook questions the appropriateness of the phrase 'hospital discharge', since this implies some sort of termination or end-point, rather than simply a transfer to community services (Henwood 1994, p. 1):

> Effective hospital discharge is dependent upon the various agencies involved acknowledging their complementary responsibilities. The benefits of getting it right can include maximising individuals' chance of recovery; improved hospital bed usage; more effective targeting of scarce assessment skills, and well informed community health staff knowing exactly what contribution they need to make to the care of the individual. The costs of getting it wrong include: a poor service to patients, and unnecessarily slow recovery; GPs not knowing what has happened to their patients; social services staff receiving inappropriate referrals; disputes breaking out; un-planned readmissions, a general waste of resources, and the risk of bad publicity on bed blocking.

> The workbook focuses primarily on discharge from hospital. However, it is also apparent that a discharge from hospital is an admission – or transfer – to community care; and an admission to hospital is a transfer from the community. It is crucial, therefore, to recognise that actions and decisions made at any point in a care episode can have consequences for other parts of the health and social care system.

In 1995, the government issued new guidance to replace its 1989 predecessor (Department of Health 1995). Although new guidance was probably long overdue following the changes introduced under the community care reforms, circular HSG(95)8/LAC(95)5 was essentially a response to a recent report by the Health Service Commissioner ('the Leeds case'). After a long-term reduction in the number of long-stay NHS beds and the 1990 Community Care Act, more and more patients who had previously been cared for by the NHS were falling under the remit of SSDs, where they had to pay for care that they had previously received free of charge. These developments are described in more detail elsewhere (*see*, for example, Glasby and Littlechild 2000a; Means and Smith 1998a; Wistow 1996), but led to a complaint from the wife of a 55-year-old man with severe brain damage who felt that her husband should receive free NHS continuing care rather than means-tested social care. The complaint was subsequently upheld, and the case generated significant controversy about national policy in this area, culminating in new government guidance.

Although most of the 1995 circular focused on continuing healthcare needs, it also contained a small section on hospital discharge. As Table 3.1 demonstrates, however, the 1995 circular was much less detailed than its 1989 counterpart and provided much less protection for patients. Whereas vulnerable patients had previously been entitled to support with transport and domestic arrangements on the day of discharge, for example, the 1995 guidance makes no mention of such issues. Similarly, whereas the 1989 circular makes direct reference to the communication needs of people at risk of not understanding their discharge arrangements, the 1995 document does not include any such safeguards. Compared to its 1989 predecessor, indeed, one of the few contributions of HSG(95)8/LAC(95)5 was to reiterate the role of the consultant in deciding when patients should be discharged and the type of care they may need. From 1995 onwards, the consultant (in consultation with others) was to decide when patients no longer need acute care and whether patients require:

- ongoing NHS care
- NHS-funded rehabilitation
- discharge to a residential or nursing home
- discharge home with a package of health and social care.

At the same time, a second key contribution was to introduce a slightly more ominous tone into hospital discharge. Although the 1989 circular had focused on the responsibilities of key members of staff and the needs of the patient, its 1995 equivalent is explicit that 'where patients have been assessed as not requiring NHS continuing inpatient care, ... they do not have the right to occupy indefinitely an NHS bed' (Department of Health 1995, p. 8). Whilst this issue is not explored in much more detail in the circular, the wording is somewhat threatening and the implication seems to be that some patients may refuse to be discharged and inappropriately occupy a hospital bed. From protecting patients likely to have ongoing support needs, therefore, policy had shifted to incorporate the view that individual patients may be 'troublemakers'. In addition, there is also a greater recognition that patients may not agree with decisions about eligibility for continuing NHS care and much of the 'hospital discharge' section of the 1995 circular focuses on this topic. Rather than guidance from a government concerned about the welfare of patients about to be discharged from hospital, therefore, HSG(95)8/LAC(95)5 reads very much as an attempt to clarify administrative responsibility for an area of care where

Table 3.1: 1989 versus 1995 guidance

Key features	1989 circular/booklet	1995 circular
Discharge procedures should be kept under review and performance should be regularly audited	X	•
Assessment of home situation to be carried out at earliest possible stage	•	X
Any support, help or equipment required should be available by the time the patient leaves hospital	•	X
Immediately necessary housing adaptations should be made (or at least a firm timetable agreed)	•	X
Importance of liaison with social services and housing if appropriate (in good time)	•	•
Patients moving to a private nursing home should be informed in writing whether the health authority will pay the fees	•	X
Patients can refuse to be discharged into a residential or nursing home	•	•
Patients and carers to be consulted and informed at every stage	•	•
Important that people with sensory impairments or mental health problems or who do not speak English as a first language understand	•	X
Written or tape-recorded material may be helpful when communication is difficult	•	X
Special action may be necessary if patients are discharged at or just before weekends or bank holidays or late in the day	•	X
Sets out specific roles for all key workers	•	X
Medical team to discuss with patient likely outcome of admission, length of stay and future support needs	•	X
Medical team to discuss with patient, ward sister and others expected discharge date or follow-up arrangements as soon as practicable	•	X

	Col 1	Col 2
Medical team to notify patient's GP in writing of date of discharge, diagnosis, follow-up arrangements and patient management required	•	X
Plans for discharge to commence as soon as possible after admission	•	X
Importance of multidisciplinary assessment	•	•
Nursing team to ensure that arrangements have been made for transport home	•	X
For vulnerable people living alone, food should be provided and the home heated	•	X
There should be safe access to stairs or toilet and it should be possible for the patient to gain entry to their home	•	X
Importance of involvement by therapists where necessary	•	X
Social services to be involved at an early stage	•	•
At least 48 hours notice of discharge to be given if possible	•	X
Consultant, in consultation with other key staff, responsible for deciding when someone no longer needs acute care	•	•
Consultant, in consultation with others, decides most appropriate response to patient's needs (e.g. NHS care, rehabilitation, discharge)	X	•
Younger people not to be inappropriately placed in care homes for older people	X	•
Patients moving into a care home can choose which home (within limits on cost and assessed needs)	X	•
When there is no vacancy in a chosen home, the patient may need to be discharged to another home until a place becomes available	X	•
Unless they qualify for NHS continuing inpatient care, patients do not have a right to occupy an NHS bed indefinitely	X	•
Sets out detailed arrangements for reviewing or appealing decisions about eligibility for NHS continuing care	X	•

X = not included in document; • = included in document.

the powers that be are expecting trouble. Although this is probably under-standable in light of the controversy generated by the Leeds case, the impres-sion remains that the 1995 guidance was a retrograde step for hospital discharge.

In 1996, policy guidance accompanying the Carers (Recognition and Services) Act 1995 made a specific reference to the needs and rights of carers during the discharge process. The Act gave those providing care to a person being assessed for community care services or services for children the right, on request, to an assessment of their needs, on condition that they are providing a substantial amount of care on a regular basis (Department of Health 1996, p. 5):

> ... the Act covers those carers who are about to take on substantial and regular caring tasks for someone who has just become, or is becoming, disabled through accident or physical or mental ill health. Local and health authorities will need to ensure that hospital discharge procedures take account of the provisions of the Act and that carers are involved once planning for discharge starts.

While the 1995 Act was the first piece of carers' legislation, subsequent mon-itoring and research suggest that its impact has sometimes been limited. This has been dealt with in more detail elsewhere, but evidence reveals that many carers are not informed about their rights under the Act and do not receive written results of their assessment (Carers National Association 1997). Against this background, the inclusion of a reference to hospital discharge in the policy guidance, though important, was prob-ably never going to revolutionise carers' experience of the discharge process (*see* Chapters 4 and 5 for specific examples of research into carers and hospital discharge).

In 1997, academics from the School for Public Policy at the University of Bristol published a workbook designed to promote partnership working between health, social care and housing (Means *et al.* 1997). Produced in conjunction with the Department of Health and the Department of the Environment, Transport and the Regions, the workbook was produced with the aid of a steering group and a practitioner panel. Although most of the workbook focused on issues such as joint working, assessment and care management, home adaptation or improvement and the relationship between primary care and housing, the final module addressed hospital admission and discharge, emphasising the importance of the often-neglected housing dimensions of hospital discharge. After setting the housing policy context (what hospital social services staff need to know about housing), the workbook explains what housing staff need to know about hospitals and hospital discharge. Next, the authors discuss general issues for oper-ational staff, highlight some examples of good practice and consider more specialist issues, such as mental health.

In many ways, the 1997 housing workbook was similar to the 1994 hospital discharge workbook discussed above:

- both were officially sponsored workbooks making an important contribution to neglected and complex areas of practice
- both were produced by leading academics with input from a wide range of policy-makers and practitioners
- both emphasise good practice that, if implemented, would significantly improve the quality of care experienced by service users.

Despite this, both workbooks also share the same underlying limitation: without decisive government action, the good practice espoused by Henwood (1994) and Means *et al.* (1997) (*see* Box 3.5) remains optional rather than mandatory, and there is no guarantee that either workbook will be put into practice.

Box 3.5 The importance of housing

Housing is crucial to hospital discharge because:

- Adequate housing is an essential contributor to good health
- Provision, adaptation and renovation of suitable housing are key components of a system of comprehensive care
- … An individual who has undergone a major life change with illness may find it triggers a change in housing need …
- With regard to older people, there is a risk of inappropriate discharge, particularly where the patient or family/friends may have unrealistic expectations about care delivery in the sheltered or extra care environment or where the additional care requirements may be outside the existing contract between the housing provider and social services

From service users' point of view, the need for attention to the housing dimension of hospital … discharge is very clear because:

- there is a risk that their stay in hospital will be prolonged
- there is a risk that they will have to be readmitted.

Source: Means *et al.* 1997, p. 100

Looking back at the community care reforms, it seems likely that the government of the day did not fully appreciate the significance that their polices were likely to have for hospital discharge and that their handling of this issue was inadequate. With the benefit of hindsight, it is easy to be critical of the failure of the 1989 circular to take account of imminent changes in policy and practice (*see* Chapter 2) and the superficial coverage of hospital discharge in the community care guidance. Despite action at the eleventh hour in 1991 and 1992, the decision to compel local and health authorities to agree how to integrate hospital discharge procedures and assessment arrangements seems all too little too late. Even during the mid-1990s, official responses were ultimately unsatisfactory and left what some may see as an unacceptable amount to local discretion.

• Although the 1994 and 1997 workbooks were an important contribution, the good practice guidance offered was no substitute for decisive central action to combat the problematic nature of hospital discharge head-on.
• Despite new guidance in 1995, circular HSG(95)8/LAC(95)5 was much less detailed than its 1989 predecessor and seems more of an attempt to clarify administrative responsibilities than the product of a genuine desire to improve the hospital discharges experienced by patients.
• Whilst references to the needs of carers in the policy guidance to the Carers (Recognition and Services) Act 1995 are to be welcomed, subsequent evidence suggests that even the most basic elements of the Act were not always successfully implemented and progress has been slow (*see also* Chapters 4 and 5).

In the absence of a strong central lead, therefore, it was always going to fall to local health and social care agencies to make hospital discharge arrangements work (or not as the case may be) (*see below* and Chapters 4 and 5).

The health and social care divide under New Labour

In 1997, Tony Blair's New Labour party was elected by a landslide majority after 18 years in opposition. Eager to make their mark, the new government pledged to 'hit the ground running' and embarked upon an ambitious process of reform with remarkable speed. Early measures included the granting of independence to the Bank of England to set interest rates (Thomas 2001) and the creation of a Royal Commission on Long Term Care (1999). In health and social care, the rate and pace of change was initially slower, but after a cautious start quickly became substantial, with a series of consultation documents, green papers and white papers seemingly set to revolutionise service provision (*see* Box 3.6).

Box 3.6   Which Blair project? New Labour and the health–social care divide

- *Winter pressures* money to reduce the pressures faced by health and social care over the winter months (Department of Health 1997a, 1997b) (*see* Chapter 6 for further details)
- A *Better Services for Vulnerable People* initiative to introduce joint investment plans for continuing and community care services, improve multi-disciplinary assessment and promote independence through timely recuperation and rehabilitation opportunities (Department of Health 1997c)
- A *partnership grant* (totalling nearly £650 million over three years) (Department of Health 1998b)
- *Health improvement programmes* to improve local health and health care (Department of Health 1997d)
- *Health action zones* to improve the health of local people via locally agreed strategies (Department of Health 1997d)
- *Primary care groups or trusts* (with social services representation on the governing body) (Department of Health 1997d)
- *National Service Frameworks* to improve the quality and consistency of health and social care services (Department of Health 1997d)
- New *integrated community equipment stores* (Department of Health 2001a)
- New powers to promote joint working announced in the *Partnership in Action* consultation document and subsequently enacted in *The Health Act 1999* (Department of Health 1998a; 1999b). This initiative is described in more detail in Chapter 6
- New *care trusts* (providing both health and social care) can be established under the *Health and Social Care Act 2001* (Department of Health 2001b, 2001c)
- A *single assessment process* for older people so that they do not have to undergo several different assessments by several different health and social care practitioners, each asking for similar information (Department of Health 2001d)
- Increased emphasis on *intermediate care* (Department of Health 2001e) to prevent unnecessary hospital admissions, facilitate swift hospital discharges and prevent premature admission to residential or nursing homes (*see* Chapter 6)
- The creation of four new *regional directors of health and social care* (Department of Health 2001f)

Often, the scope of such policy initiatives has made it difficult for practitioners to keep up with the pace of change. Faced with a plethora of circulars and policy documents, most front-line workers simply are not able to keep abreast of all the latest developments. Hearing of a new policy initiative, obtaining a copy, reading it, assimilating the proposals and making a considered response all takes time, and time is a precious commodity. For many workers, there simply are not enough hours in the day to balance familiarising oneself with new policy developments with the day-to-day demands of the job. As a result, the majority of practitioners have little choice but to continue with their work, only half aware of changes from the centre which might one day come to revolutionise the way in which they work in the future (Glasby and Littlechild 2000c).

Throughout New Labour's time in office, a key aim has been to bring down what has been described as the 'Berlin Wall' which separates health and social care (House of Commons Debates 1997). Specific initiatives are set out in Box 3.6 above and have been described in more detail elsewhere (*see* Chapter 6 for specific examples, and Glasby and Littlechild (2000a) for a chronological overview). However, a key theme of New Labour's approach has been a refusal to sanction wholesale reorganisation of the existing system and a marked preference for a more subtle and incremental process of change. Thus, the *Partnership in Action* consultation document specifically ruled out major reorganisation of health and social care on the grounds that it would be extremely disruptive without necessarily improving the quality of front-line services (Department of Health 1998a, p. 5):

> Major structural change is not the answer. We do not intend to set up new statutory health and social services authorities. They would involve new bureaucracy and would be expensive and disruptive to introduce. Our proposals set out a better course which is less bureaucratic and more efficient for users, for carers, and for staff working in those services who are often as frustrated as the people they are trying to help by the failures of the system.

Instead, the document and subsequent policy initiatives focused on a more gradual blurring of the boundaries between health and social care, removing some of the existing barriers to joint working and encouraging greater inter-agency collaboration by a combination of incentives and central compulsion. Key developments include winter pressures funding, 'flexibilities' introduced under the Health Act 1999, intermediate care and care trusts (*see* Box 3.6 above and Chapter 6 for further details). Although many of these initiatives will inevitably affect hospital discharge, however, there have been few policies that make direct reference to this area of practice. Even those documents that do mention discharge, tend to make only broad statements about the issue without necessarily setting out the details of how the government's statements are to be achieved (*see* Box 3.7 for examples).

Box 3.7   Generalised statements on hospital discharge

Many carers have expressed concern about lack of recognition of the role of the carers in hospital settings. At the time of hospital discharge, carers must be fully informed and involved in the planning of future care of the patient, so that assumptions are not made about their ability or willingness to care. Studies of carers' views of hospital discharge highlight particular difficulties about failure to involve them in the timing of discharge and to give them enough information about the future care of the patient.

Source: Department of Health 1999c, p. 40

We will introduce new standards to ensure that every patient has a discharge plan including an assessment of their care needs, developed from the beginning of their hospital admission.

Source: Department of Health 2000a, p. 102

Although these statements are to be welcomed, there is very little detail as to how such pledges will work in practice.

Despite a lack of emphasis on hospital discharge in many New Labour policy initiatives, however, a 1997 circular *has* highlighted the need to update current guidance on hospital discharge (Department of Health 1997c, Annex A). Whilst this recognition is to be welcomed in light of the inadequacies of the 1995 circular (*see above*), action has not yet followed at the time of writing (late 2002). In June 2001, the Department of Health issued new guidance on continuing care, replacing circular HSG(95)8/LAC(95)5 (Department of Health 2001g). After a number of changes in health and social care, and a high-profile legal case (Department of Health 1999a), the 2001 document was designed to consolidate previous guidance in light of new developments. Unfortunately, the circular focused almost entirely on the issue of NHS responsibilities for continuing care and NHS services for people in residential or nursing homes, neglecting to mention hospital discharge at all. At first glance, this would appear to be something of an oversight on two main grounds:

1 Circular HSG(95)8/LAC(95)5 expired on 1 March 2000, yet new guidance was not produced until the end of June 2001, 16 months later.
2 The 2001 circular cancelled previous guidance on hospital discharge and continuing care, yet only covered continuing care, leaving something of a vacuum as far as discharge is concerned.

Technically, therefore, the NHS and local authorities did not have any guidance at all on hospital discharge and continuing care between March

2000 and June 2001 and, at the time of writing, still do not have any guidance for hospital discharge. As in 1995, it is interesting to note that the circular in question was a response to a high-profile legal case and it seems likely that the government's attention was once again on preventing future legal difficulties rather than on improving hospital discharge practices (*see above*).

More recently, the government has launched three key policy measures that are likely to have significant implications for hospital discharge.

Measure 1

In October 2001, the Department of Health announced an additional £300 million to be distributed over two years to help end widespread 'bed blocking' (Department of Health 2001h). Targeted in part towards 50 local authorities experiencing particular difficulties in this area, the money was described as a 'cash for change' initiative, linking the new investment with changes outlined in a separate document on developing partnerships between the public and independent sectors (Department of Health 2001i). As part of this policy initiative, a new Change Agent Team was established to help improve hospital discharge arrangements and to encourage a single system of health and social care (Department of Health 2002a). According to Health Secretary, Alan Milburn (Department of Health 2001h):

> Bed-blocking is a major problem for all NHS patients. Bed-blocking leaves people in beds who should be cared for elsewhere and keeps people from beds who need treatment straight away. We are determined to tackle this problem which has bedevilled the health service for decades so that patients receive the right care in the right place at the right time.

At the time of writing it is too early to tell how this policy initiative will work in practice. However, whilst additional funding to tackle 'bed-blocking' must surely be welcomed, it is difficult to see how a sudden and relatively short-term injection of funding can resolve all of the deep-seated problems described at various stages throughout this book at once (*see* Glasby (2002a) for more detailed discussion).

Measure 2

In May 2002, the Chancellor announced 'the largest ever sustained increase in NHS funding' (Department of Health 2002b, p. 10). Funded by an increase in national insurance (NI) contributions, the government pledged a 7.5% annual real terms increase in NHS spending for five years, with a 6% per year real terms growth in social care over three years. However, these new funding arrangements were to be accompanied by a new system of 'cross-charging'. Building on the Swedish and Danish systems, the government has signalled its intention to legislate in order to charge SSDs for hospital beds 'blocked' by people medically fit for discharge. Although full details are still to be finalised, it seems as though those departments who reduce the number of 'blocked beds' will be able to use the new money for other services, whereas those who cannot secure discharges within an agreed timescale will be charged for keeping patients in hospital unnecessarily. To reduce the likelihood of premature discharges, this new policy will be accompanied by charges on NHS hospitals for emergency hospital readmissions (Department of Health 2002b, p. 33; *see also* Department of Health 2002d):

> We have been impressed by the success of the system in countries like Sweden and Denmark in getting delayed discharges from hospital down. We intend to legislate therefore to introduce a similar system of cross-charging. The new social services cash … includes resources to cover the cost of beds needlessly blocked in hospitals through delayed discharges … If councils reduce the number of blocked beds, they will have the freedom to use these resources to invest in alternative social care services. If they cannot meet the agreed time limit they will be charged by the local hospital for the cost it incurs in keeping older people in hospital unnecessarily. In this way there will be far stronger incentives in the system to ensure that patients do not have to experience long delays in their discharge from hospital. There will be matching incentive charges on NHS hospitals to make them responsible for the costs of emergency hospital readmissions, so as to ensure patients are not discharged prematurely.

Whilst action to tackle delayed discharges is urgently needed, the government's latest announcement has a number of flaws (*see*, for example, Clode 2002; Glasby 2002d, 2002e; Glendinning 2002; House of Commons Health Committee 2002).

- The charges threaten to distort SSD priorities – if departments can be charged for 'bed blocking' there will be a very real incentive to focus on reducing delayed discharges at the expense of other important services. This might include a range of vulnerable user groups, such as children or people with learning difficulties. Conceivably, charging could even lead to a greater number of hospital admissions, as some SSDs may choose to focus on facilitating swift discharge rather than on preventative measures to stop people being admitted to hospital in the first place.
- It is by no means clear as to whether the extra money for SSDs will be adequate. Although 6% is undoubtedly welcome, many departments feel that they have been chronically underfunded for many years and that even more investment will be required. In addition, the Department of Health has made it clear that the extra money will also have to be spent on increasing care home fees in order to stabilise the residential or nursing home market. Add this to the fact that local government will

face substantially higher costs as a result of the Chancellor's increase in NI and a seemingly generous package begins to lose its initial appeal.

- Delayed hospital discharge is a complex issue and has a range of causes. Research to date suggests that 'bed blocking' can sometimes be the fault of SSDs, but that it can also be the result of internal hospital delays or of factors outside the control of either health or social care (*see* Chapters 4 and 5).
- Different countries have different priorities and problems, and their healthcare systems have tended to evolve over time in response to the local context. As a result, there is no guarantee that a policy imported from one country will be successful in another. Sweden, for example, is very different from the UK in a range of areas, not least in the fact that its healthcare is provided through local government rather than through a separate NHS.

Above all, however, charging threatens to damage the new relationships which health and social services are beginning to develop. Partnership working is a key government priority, and it is difficult to see how a policy that encourages one agency to blame another for local problems is going to help organisations work constructively together.

Measure 3

In July 2002, the Health Secretary announced a package of measures to improve services for older people (Department of Health 2002c). Key pledges included the following.

- *Faster assessment of need*: by the end of 2004, assessments will begin within 48 hours and be complete within one month. Following assessment, services will be provided within one month. All equipment to help people live independently in their own homes will be provided within one week.
- *More support to help more people who need care in residential and nursing homes*: extra resources will enable local authorities to pay higher fees for this type of care and stabilise the local care home market. Recent national standards about environmental conditions (for example, the availability of single rooms and the number of lifts and baths) will become good practice guidance rather than mandatory. Funding of £70 million will be made available by 2006 to support training for social care staff.
- *Greater choice*: an expansion of rehabilitation services and extra-care sheltered housing.
- *More people will receive support to continue living at home*: an increase in intensive help to remain at home and the abolition of charges for community equipment, such as hand rails or hoists from April 2003.

- *An expansion of direct payments*: previously optional, direct payments will become mandatory, enabling older people to choose between directly provided services or a cash payment to purchase their own care (*see* Glasby and Littlechild, 2002 for further details on direct payments).
- *Support for carers*: the current Carers Grant will double by 2006, providing the support required for people to continue in their role as carers.

Although all these proposals are to be welcomed in principle, major doubts must remain about the feasibility of achieving such dramatic change within such tight timescales. In spite of increased funding for social care, it seems as though the commitments of SSDs may increase at a much greater rate than their budgets, and it is difficult to see how departments will be able to deliver these challenging targets.

Overall, therefore, New Labour's contribution to hospital discharge has probably been more constructive than its Conservative predecessor, but there is still a long way to go. Despite numerous changes and a wide range of initiatives designed to promote closer joint working between health and social care, New Labour has sometimes tended to overwhelm front-line practitioners with the scale and pace of its initiatives and has introduced few specific policies regarding hospital discharge. Following a high-profile legal case, moreover, previous guidance on hospital discharge (albeit inadequate) has been allowed to expire without being updated or replaced. More recently, there has been a flurry of initiatives likely to have a significant effect upon hospital discharge, but little evidence that the measures proposed will be successful in improving the current situation. Although partnership working may now be more firmly on the political agenda and practitioners are able to work more flexibly together, hospital discharge remains a problematic area of service provision and continues to represent a major area of tension on the fault line between health and social care. That this is the case is demonstrated in more detail in Chapters 4 and 5.

Summary

In Chapter 2 we have seen how securing effective and co-ordinated hospital discharges can be crucial, both for patients and for service providers:

- hospital beds are expensive and delayed discharges waste scarce public resources
- delayed discharges can prevent the admission of other patients who require hospital care
- hospital is often an unsuitable environment for people fit for discharge, and unnecessarily prolonged hospital stays can lead to the patient contracting a hospital-acquired infection or losing their independence.

Despite this, many of the policy initiatives summarised above have been deeply unsatisfactory in three main respects:

1 Central government has often overlooked the importance of hospital discharge. Thus, there has been relatively little guidance on this topic over the years and the guidance that has been produced has not always been satisfactory. Key examples include the lengthy gap between the 1963 and 1989 circulars, the failure of the 1989 circular to refer to the community care reforms and the failure of New Labour to replace the lapsed 1995 guidance.

2 Central government has tended to leave hospital discharge to local discretion, requiring local agencies to develop their own policies and protocols for dealing with the difficult issues that joint working can raise. Examples of this process include the 1992 December 31st Agreements as well as a host of New Labour policies described above and in Chapter 6.

3 Much central intervention has been based on good practice guidance and on exhortations to further partnership working aimed at individual workers and local agencies, with very little attempt to tackle the structural obstacles to joint working. While welcome, the 1994 and 1997 workbooks were not sufficient to guarantee improvements in hospital discharge practices across the country and were not an adequate substitute for decisive government action. This distinction between individual, organisational and structural issues is one to which this book returns in Chapters 5–7.

CHAPTER 4

Research findings I

Throughout the various debates and new initiatives discussed in Chapters 2 and 3, the problematic nature of hospital discharge has been highlighted in a series of key studies. Of course, approximately 5.8 million people are admitted to hospital every year (House of Commons Select Committee on Public Accounts 2001) and most are discharged with few if any problems. However, a substantial minority – especially those with complex needs that span traditional service boundaries – have consistently been found to experience poorly co-ordinated and inadequate discharges. Against this background, Chapters 4 and 5 review available research and other material in order to consider the evidence for the problematic nature of hospital discharge. This is not a systematic review – very detailed and accessible summaries of current literature have already been produced by organisations such as the Scottish Office (Taraborrelli *et al.* 1998) and the King's Fund (Marks 1994). Instead, this section of the book seeks to highlight some of the key studies and themes in order to illustrate the longstanding and deep-seated difficulties which surround hospital discharge. As a result Chapter 4 focuses on research and other findings from the 1970s to the election of New Labour in 1997. After this, Chapter 5 turns attention to research published from 1998 onwards, to the experiences of user groups other than older people and to hospital discharge in Wales, Scotland and Northern Ireland.

The problematic nature of hospital discharge

Although hospital discharge has acquired an increased significance following the NHS and Community Care Act 1990 (*see* Chapters 2 and 3), research on this topic dates back more than 30 years. In 1975, for example, Age Concern Liverpool's Continuing Care Project found evidence to suggest that:

- services are not properly co-ordinated
- services are not clear about the limits of their responsibilities
- services are not designed with the needs of older people in mind
- information-sharing is inadequate

- different agencies do not always know what services are provided by other organisations
- staff attitudes can sometimes be unhelpful, viewing older people as a burden on already hard-pressed services.

Elsewhere, various studies have sought to identify the rate of 'blocked beds' (*see* Table 4.1) and have consistently identified a number of key themes (summarised in Tierney *et al.* 1994a, pp. 479–480):

- poor communication between hospital and community
- lack of assessment and planning for discharge
- inadequate notice of discharge
- inadequate consultation with patients and their carers
- over-reliance on informal support and lack of (or slow) statutory service provision
- inattention to the special needs of vulnerable groups, such as frail older people.

Added to this list must also be premature discharge, with some patients and health or social care practitioners feeling that individual patients have sometimes been discharged from hospital too quickly in order to make room for new patients (*see*, for example, Victor *et al.* 1993a). Another key issue that will emerge in Chapters 4 and 5 is the lack of attention often paid to the needs of carers (*see*, for example, Henwood 1998; Hill and Macgregor 2001; Holzhausen 2001).

Table 4.1:   Examples of delayed discharges*

Author(s)	Location of research	Rate of delayed discharges (%)
Rubin and Davis (1975)	Liverpool	4.8
Murphy (1977)	East London	13
Coid and Crome (1986)	Bromley	14
Namdaran *et al.* (1992)	Edinburgh	19
Victor *et al.* (1993a)	Inner London	14.6
Victor *et al.* (2000)	Three English hospitals	27

*See Appendix A for a more detailed discussion of the methodological issues raised by attempts to measure the rate of delayed discharges.

Despite the large volume of research from the 1960s and 1970s onwards, however, the bulk of Chapters 4 and 5 focuses on research from the late 1980s to 2001, summarising some of the key findings with regard to hospital discharge during the implementation and subsequent 'bedding down' of the community care reforms. In 1992, for example, the National Institute for Social Work (NISW) published Department of Health-funded research into the experiences of people aged 75 and over discharged from hospital and referred for home care services (Neill and Williams 1992). Based on data collected via a national telephone survey of local authorities, home care referrals in four SSDs, a sample of 70 older people and the views of home care organisers and home carers, the study provided an important insight into hospital discharge practice in the build up to the implementation of the NHS and Community Care Act 1990. During the telephone interviews, there was a suggestion that recent changes in health and social care had transformed the hospital discharge of older people into something of a 'hot issue'. In particular, participants were anxious about reductions in the length of hospital stays and the implications this could have for patients and for local authorities (Neill and Williams 1992, pp. 8 and 17):

> Concern was expressed that medical efficiency, influenced by waiting lists, was being measured by swift throughput of patients so that, for example, a patient might be discharged within days of major surgery, irrespective of the age and the state of health of their carer. It was considered that the pressure on old people in hospital to move out, the speed of their discharge, their vulnerable post-illness state, advanced age and lack of information raised ethical issues about their freedom of choice and their need for protection ... Overall, the changing roles of hospitals, the increased throughput of patients and the growth of private residential provision had presented social services departments with considerable unanticipated demands and challenges at all levels. The need for some elderly frail people to have a period of recovery and special care after their discharge from hospital was emphasised by the principal officers and social workers who were interviewed. However, changes in provision between health and social services meant that intensive care services for old people on their discharge were often patchily provided and seldom able to give comprehensive cover. In no local authority in 1988 was there a fully coherent policy for responding to the new situation in which people were being discharged from hospital quicker and sicker.

In addition to this, the NISW study found evidence that home care organisers sometimes received very little information about the needs of individual service users until after they had been discharged and a home care package had begun. Only 8% of referrals for home care were made before the patient was discharged home, with 18% made on the day of discharge, 56% in the week after discharge and 18% even later than one week. Of these referrals, a large number were deemed to be inappropriate by home care organisers, some of whom suggested that home care is a service that is sometimes offered automatically with little awareness about the role of home carers. When interviewed two weeks after discharge, a significant number of patients highlighted issues such as premature discharge, lack of consultation and inadequate notice of discharge (*see* Table 4.2). One in three patients experienced a good discharge and one in five patients had very poor discharge experiences, with a 'good' discharge defined in terms of the older person:

- being given at least 24 hours' notice of discharge
- being given the opportunity to discuss how they would manage after discharge
- having someone with them on the journey home
- having someone waiting for them at home
- having someone who calls to see them on the day of discharge.

Key problems for some people included long waits for transport, a lack of assistance in getting from the transport into the house and the lack of a person waiting for the patient at home. Nearly all participants were found to be severely disabled when interviewed two weeks after discharge, with many unable to leave their homes and experiencing physical pain, poor sleeping patterns and some loss of bladder control. Only one in four said they felt well and one in three people were possibly clinically depressed. In terms of formal services, the older people received an average of four hours' home care per week, although interviews with home carers suggested that over half were doing additional jobs for their service users outside of work (such as taking washing home, changing light bulbs and enlisting their husbands to carry out minor repairs and change plugs). Other domiciliary services were patchy, with particular shortfalls in chiropody and assistance with bathing (despite the fact that more than two-thirds of the older people were unable to have a bath/shower/all-over wash without help and four-fifths were unable to cut their own toe nails). When interviews were followed up 12 weeks after discharge, over half of the participants were unable to leave the house and two-fifths were experiencing severe pain, yet home care input had been reduced by an average of one-and-a-half hours per week. Although only a small number of carers (28) were interviewed as part of the study, many described personal or physical stress, physical health problems and anxiety or depression.

Table 4.2:   Older people's experiences of discharge*

Older people's experience of discharge (as reported two weeks after discharge)	Percentage of patients (n = 69)
The patient felt weak or ill on discharge	52
The patient was given one day's notice or less of discharge	40
The patient's answers indicated possible depression	35
The patient did not discuss his or her needs after discharge	35
The patient felt they were discharged too soon	24
The patient was alone all day immediately after discharge	17

*Adapted from Neill and Williams 1992, Chapters 7–9.

In addition to these specific findings, the NISW study also provided some very powerful examples of poor discharge practices and the impact of these on the lives of individual older people (*see* Box 4.1). Building on this rich data, NISW followed up its initial research with a number of workshops run in conjunction with the SSI and Regional Health Authorities (RHAs) in order to disseminate the findings of the 1992 study to health and social care practitioners. After an initial meeting to formulate goals for action at a local level, participants attended a second event three months later in order to evaluate the extent to which their goals had been achieved (Phillipson and Williams 1995). In addition to reporting on some of the key ideas developed by participants, the workshop report concluded with a useful summary of some of the key issues from a practitioner's perspective (Phillipson and Williams 1995, pp. 29–30):

> Hospital discharge straddles health and social care, hospitals, the community and individuals' homes, large scale planning and attention to individual detail. It is also a touchstone for a number of significant aspects of current practice in health and social care, such as joint working, the rights of service users, the recognition of carers' needs, and the necessity to ensure that both policy and practice recognise the needs and preferences of people from different ethnic backgrounds and cultures. While senior managers have to translate legislation and guidance into local policies, it is practitioners who have to translate these into everyday practice. As such they are in a key position to know how effective the policies are for individual service users and patients. Just as it is imperative to seek out and listen to the experiences of service users, so too it is important to ask practitioners 'how is it going?'... The combined messages from participants who read and commented on this report were:
>
> - keep the person – be they patient, service user or carer – central
> - bring together the people who are responsible for all the different aspects of the discharge
> - although hospital discharge is complex, the process should be kept as simple as possible
> - give practitioners an avenue to comment on and change policies which are ineffective
> - managers need to open ways of enabling practitioner views and ideas to be listened to and acted upon.

Box 4.1 Leaving hospital: elderly people and their discharge to community care

'I didn't know what was going to happen to me – what they were going to do – where I would be sent. I don't want to end up in one of those geriatric places.'

continued overleaf

'I was given lots of medicine and tablets when I was discharged but I was not told what they were for. I was just given the name and the label. I still do not know what these tablets are for ... It would be nice if people took the time to explain things a lot more when you are in hospital.'

... The sample included another lady who had had a leg amputated, who was confined to a wheelchair and lived alone. A trial home visit had been planned but was cancelled because the ambulance did not arrive. The following day she was discharged home without a trial visit as her hospital bed was needed ... Two weeks after discharge [the woman] was found to be in pain, and depressed. She was unable to reach her kitchen cupboards at all and struggled to reach her taps from her wheelchair because the sink needed adjusting. She had to reach over her cooker to the controls which were on a panel at the back. Her bed was too high and her armchair too low. She badly needed help to get in and out of bed. This person had no relatives, some contact with her neighbours but no regular help at weekends during which time her commode was unemptied. Her ... home help sometimes called, in unpaid time during the weekend, to empty the commode.

'I [a discharge scheme co-ordinator] happened to call into the ward and the charge nurse told me that they had sent her (the patient) home that morning because they needed the bed, but the nurse said the patient would be alright because they had given her a packed lunch to take with her. I was worried so I called in to see her on my way home from work. I don't know what would have happened if I had not called. She had no food or milk and was feeling too weak and tired to get into bed or into the kitchen. She had plenty of neighbours and friends to help, but they did not know she was home. She had no phone and was too weak to go out to them.'

Source: Neill and Williams 1992, pp. 57, 67–68 and 81–82

Also in 1992, an Audit Commission report on the use of medical beds in acute hospitals found evidence that internal administrative issues and delays in securing community or institutional care packages were causing delays in discharges for patients otherwise able to return home (Audit Commission 1992, p. 1):

Discharge procedures are often poorly organized. There are frequent delays in arranging transport and take-home medicines as well as longer delays because of the need to organise domiciliary support. Discharges are sometimes also delayed because residential or nursing placements cannot easily be found.

Key issues included:

- delays in ordering, dispensing and distributing take-home medicines
- delays in obtaining transport and inappropriate referrals for ambulances when a hospital car would suffice
- poor communication with the patient, the GP and outside agencies
- poorly planned and managed packages of care for people returning home from hospital
- delays in arranging home care
- the availability of residential and nursing home places
- problematic relationships between hospitals and SSDs (including social workers failing to attend discharge planning meetings and a lack of incentives for social workers to facilitate swift discharge).

In the same year, the SSI published findings from its inspections of hospital social services teams in five SSDs and a survey of staff providing services to health sites (Department of Health/SSI 1992a, 1992b, 1993). These suggested that approximately 20% of social services fieldwork social work staff (including managers) were involved in health-related social work – a substantial proportion of the whole workforce. Although all five authorities recognised the importance of multi-disciplinary working, only one had implemented a joint discharge policy as required under government guidance (*see* Chapter 2). Whereas the inspectors felt that discharge planning seemed to work well in practice (despite the absence of formal procedures), there were areas of concern. In one hospital, there were felt to be 'too many "Friday afternoon" referrals for discharge', and another respondent commented that it was no longer necessary to keep a record of 'dangerous discharges' (presumably meaning that at one stage, discharge practices were considered to be dangerous!) (both quotes Department of Health/SSI 1992a, p. 25). There was also considerable confusion about the role of social services staff in situations where patients were being discharged straight from hospital into independent sector residential care. Thus, one authority was politically opposed to the use of the private sector, whereas others did not involve themselves in such cases or provided information and advice only. Rather worryingly, many staff interviewed were uncertain about the implications of the community care reforms for their role and did not feel as if they had been given sufficient information about the changes.

Building on this initial inspection, the SSI carried out further work in three of the original authorities to explore the experiences of users and carers (Department of Health/SSI 1993). Drawing on interviews with 59 discharged hospital patients and 26 of their carers, the report found that more than two-thirds of participants did not receive any written or verbal information about what to expect from hospital social services, their priorities or how to gain access to services, with many relying instead upon information from relatives, from community nurses prior to admission or from previous hospital stays. Many people were confused as to the role of hospital social workers and some users had little recollection of their first contact with social services staff owing to their medical condition. Most users and carers were referred to social services by ward staff, although they were often not aware that a referral had been made. Discussion with a social worker about arrangements for leaving hospital took place at various stages, with 11 individuals discussing after-care arrangements on the day before discharge and three individuals on the day of discharge itself. Less than a quarter of users were aware of any meetings taking place to discuss their support needs and many carers felt that they were not consulted about the amount of support they could provide after discharge. On preparing to leave hospital, more than half of the users interviewed received less than three days' notice of discharge and a substantial minority (less than one-quarter) were discharged on a Friday or at the weekend. Six users did not receive the services they expected to receive on arriving home and many were unaware of the complaints procedure or of their right to have access to their records. Whilst most people experienced few problems on returning home, the inspectors quoted the example of a 90-year-old visually impaired woman who was discharged on a Friday and saw no one till the following Monday. Two weeks later, she was admitted to residential care. Overall, the report recommended that (Department of Health/SSI 1993, pp. 3–4):

- [Local authorities] need to ensure that their hospital discharge procedures and arrangements should achieve an integrated approach between local hospital provision, social services and community health care.
- Statutory agencies need to be sensitive in recognising and supporting all those relatives, neighbours and friends who provide care on an informal basis without exploiting their goodwill.
- Service providers should ensure they are sufficiently flexible to produce a service geared to individual need.
- [Local authorities] need to develop ways of keeping a high public profile on areas such as the complaints procedure and client access to records.

In 1993, the Department of Health (in conjunction with the Nuffield Institute for Health Community Care Division) published a study of hospital discharge arrangements in six English localities where such arrangements were believed to be well advanced (Henwood and Wistow 1993). Before the NHS and Community Care Act 1990, some localities had experienced difficulties such as poor communication between hospitals and social services, sometimes resulting in situations like discharges on a Friday afternoon without advance notification. Sometimes, discharges had been conducted by the hospital alone without reference to social services, with a hospital placement officer organising independent sector residential or nursing care. Thus, in one area 'the consultants simply tell a nurse to fix it up and the DSS would pay' (Henwood and Wistow 1993, p. 15). As the community care reforms were introduced, hospitals had to rely on social services conducting individual assessments before a residential or nursing placement could begin. This was more problematic in some areas of acute care than in others (Henwood and Wistow 1993, p. 16):

> Where problems had arisen in the very early days after April 1st 1993, these had generally occurred on acute medical and surgical wards. Such problems had resulted from discharges taking place without any consultation with social services ... and in [one case study site] there had been difficulties with resistance from particular consultants. The evidence suggests that a far greater shift of culture is required from those working on such wards (especially from consultants) than on wards where there is a tradition of multidisciplinary working around hospital discharge. Those who are unfamiliar with this approach are more likely to be concerned about the changes which will occur, and particularly about the potential loss of direct control over discharge and the possible consequences of 'blocked beds'.

Also apparent during the implementation of the community care reforms was an increase in paperwork and bureaucracy as, in the words of one respondent, the system moved from an informal approach 'based on trust and handshakes, to one based on project management and formal protocols'. In one area, a social work manager described the way in which practitioners were required to complete 17 pieces of paper to make a nursing home placement, likening this to 'something from the "theatre of the absurd", or like being stuck in a Kafka novel' (Henwood and Wistow 1993, p. 16). In some cases, however, this criticism of unnecessary paperwork may have been the result of a more deep-seated objection to change and to a loss of control over the discharge process. As one participant suggested (Henwood and Wistow 1993, p. 17):

> A lot of our consultants have short tempers, and they are used to doing their rounds and saying that a person should go, and not expecting them to be in the bed next time they pass. And that will be a shock.

Although all localities had a history of good relations between health and social care, the 1989 government circulars seemed to have had relatively little effect on the agencies concerned. As a result, the development of hospital discharge procedures was generally in an evolutionary state, with participants working to establish arbitration mechanisms, data collection systems and audit processes. While all six localities recognised the need to avoid unnecessary delays in hospital discharge, some areas were reluctant to commit themselves to specific targets until the new system had bedded down. Factors facilitating good practice were felt to include a good history of joint working and joint approaches to training and information cascading.

Factors hindering progress included concerns about the legality of joint commissioning, funding problems, the lack of emphasis on hospital discharge during the community care reforms (*see* Chapters 2 and 3) and the difficulty of involving GPs and consultants in training.

Whilst the 1993 study provides a detailed snapshot of activity during the implementation of the community care reforms, its central message is that hospital discharge involves two competing notions of good practice that may ultimately be incompatible (Henwood and Wistow 1993, pp. 6, 21–22 and 36–37):

> In several localities there was particular concern over potentially conflicting perspectives on good practice in hospital discharge. The prime concern of hospitals was with maintaining early discharge, in order to avoid problems with 'blocked beds', and consequent difficulties with waiting list pressures. Such concerns are clearly underpinned and reinforced by health service financial management, business plans and contracts, which also assume rapid throughput. However, definitions of good practice which are based on principles of assessment and planned discharge may conflict with these objectives.

> [In one locality] a social services respondent rejected a definition of discharge success which took account solely of health service concerns: '… they seem to see success defined in terms of not causing any embarrassment to the acute medical sector. There are other issues to consider – such as about the needs of users and carers.'

> Perhaps the most fundamental issue arises from the potential tension between two competing notions of good practice. On the one hand, a perspective which is narrowly concerned with the most cost effective use of hospital resources (and hence with rapid through-put); and on the other one which emphasises the importance of needs-led assessments and choice for individuals. The new arrangements [for community care] bring this tension into sharp relief.

> [As one participant observed] 'There has also been a marked reluctance to allow people to go and visit homes before they make a final decision. They are making one of the most important decisions of their lives, and they are expected just to do it. You have to give some people space to make decisions like that. That is why we have absolutely refused to tie down any time target for actual placements. We agreed timetables for completing assessments, but I am not going to get caught up in length of stay issues … What I am not going to have is people complaining that blocked beds are our fault … Those are not the criteria we should be judged against. I think we need to be looking at getting the service much closer to what the client wants.'

> There were conflicting perspectives on what constituted success in hospital discharge. The principal tension, which was observed to a lesser or greater extent in all localities, was between a narrowly defined resource management model, and one which might be described as user-centred. We would argue that a definition of success needs to encompass elements of both perspectives. Discharges need to be timely, and should not be delayed unnecessarily, but should also be undertaken at the pace which best suits the needs and wishes of the individual. This synthesis of perspectives requires a greater degree of change within the approach

currently dominated by resource efficiency concerns. For the acute hospital sector in particular this will require a substantial cultural change, and the development of a more holistic approach towards the care of individuals. This also requires an awareness of outcomes which are not defined solely in terms of processes or service activity levels, but in terms of the quality of life for the individual concerned.

In addition to the research of Henwood and Wistow (1993) in England, the same year also saw the publication of a series of research reports and articles on hospital discharge by the Nursing Research Unit at the University of Edinburgh. Commissioned by the Chief Scientific Officer, Scottish Office Home and Health Department, the research involved three national surveys of:

- current discharge planning in 319 Scottish acute hospital wards (Tierney *et al.* 1993b)
- the views and experiences of 1057 community nursing staff (Worth *et al.* 1993)
- the views and experiences of 311 GPs (Macmillan *et al.* 1993).

Although there were relatively few 'blocked beds' identified during the study and whereas there were many examples of good practice, participants were able to identify a range of factors that they felt frustrated the hospital discharge process or which had contributed to a negative discharge experience (*see* Box 4.2). Overall, the researchers concluded that (Tierney *et al.* 1994a, p. 489):

> The survey of 319 wards in acute hospitals throughout Scotland provides evidence that there is active attention being given to the development of discharge planning policy and practice. Although ward sisters and charge nurses hold a generally positive view of current discharge practice, they also recognise the existence and persistence of problems. From the perspective of community nursing staff and GPs, however, current discharge practice – particularly in the area of communication of information – is far from satisfactory and, with minimal direct involvement in pre-discharge planning, their community experience and knowledge of individual patients is not being used fully in the development of 'good' discharge practice and the formulation of discharge policy.

As a result, the research authors made a series of recommendations to improve hospital discharge policy and practice (Tierney *et al.* 1994a, pp. 489–490):

- A systematic approach to discharge planning should be more widely adopted and, to assist this, every ward should have a written discharge policy, key discharge standards and a discharge planning proforma for multidisciplinary use.
- For each patient there should be a named member of staff designated to assume responsibility for co-ordinating each patient's discharge planning. Nurses are well placed to assume this role.
- Patients and relatives/carers should know which member of staff is responsible for co-ordinating their discharge planning; be more regularly

and more fully involved in discharge decision-making; be given sufficient notice of the proposed discharge date; and be supplied with information about medication and continuing treatment and care.

- General practitioners and community nurses (particularly district nurses) should be directly involved at an early stage in discharge planning for patients with whom they have had prior contact and/or will be providing continuing care in the post-discharge period.
- There is a real need for improved communication and liaison between hospital and community staff ...
- Improvements are needed in the speed of delivery and the information content of the discharge summary and subsequent discharge letter [sent by the hospital to the GP].
- A stronger orientation of discharge planning towards the special needs and problems of elderly people should be developed.
- Known persistent problems surrounding hospital discharge should be investigated and resolved (in particular, widespread problems with the transport of patients home).
- Every ward should have at least a basic system of audit and quality control of hospital discharge practice and procedures.
- The outcomes and cost-effectiveness of systematic discharge planning require to be assessed through further research.

Box 4.2   Professionals' views of problematic hospital discharges

Ward staff: examples of factors that frustrate the discharge process

- Transport problems
- Inadequate notice of discharge
- Failure in provision of needed services
- Pre-discharge prescription or medication problems
- Difficulties with relatives

Source: adapted from Tierney *et al.* 1993b, p. 54

Community nurses: features indicative of unsatisfactory discharge

- Lack of support service provision
- Lack of communication between hospital and primary healthcare team
- Lack of aids/equipment/dressings/drugs
- Lack of notice or liaison regarding discharge
- Evening/weekend/holiday discharges

Source: adapted from Worth *et al.* 1993, p. 30

continued opposite

GPs: features indicative of unsatisfactory discharge

- Items related to medical condition
- Problems of mobility
- Problem related to treatment
- Mentally not able to cope
- Housing problems

Source: adapted from Macmillan *et al.* 1993, p. 32

As part of their ongoing research, the Edinburgh team also sought to explore the hospital discharge experiences of older patients and their carers (*see*, for example, Tierney *et al.* 1993a, 1994b). After a preliminary study to resolve the practicalities of patient recruitment and proforma design, the researchers interviewed 326 older patients and 117 of their carers (Tierney *et al.* 1994b). Altogether, nearly one-fifth of patients and just under one-third of carers felt that the patient was unready for discharge, citing factors such as continuing symptoms, feeling weak and tired and feeling the need for a longer period of care before discharge. As with other studies cited in Chapters 4 and 5 of this book, other key issues included a lack of notice of discharge, lack of information and lack of involvement in discharge planning (*see* Table 4.3). Crucially, there was a major difference of opinion between practitioners and patients, with the vast majority of hospital nursing staff claiming that patients are routinely given information about their follow-up care and treatment (Tierney *et al.* 1993a). This contrasted strongly with the views of patients – approximately half of whom felt that they received no information at all on any topic prior to discharge – and suggests that patients and those responsible for their care perceive the discharge process in different ways. Overall, the researchers estimated that (Tierney *et al.* 1994b, p. 37):

> ... almost 10% of the older patients in the sample were discharged from hospital with no specific planning and were informed only on the day of discharge.

In 1994, the King's Fund Institute published a review of hospital discharge as part of a series of research reports on current health issues (Marks 1994). In an introduction, the review began by emphasising the age-old nature of problems associated with hospital discharge (Marks 1994, p. 7):

> Hospital discharge arrangements involve bridging the gap between hospital and home. Discharge is a cipher for the organisational integrity of the NHS and indicates difficulties involved in implementing policies which span both hospital and community sectors. Concern over the discontinuities of care across hospital and community services has characterised the NHS since its inception and is reflected in current debates over how best to achieve seamfree – or seamless – care ... The large body of literature [on hospital discharge] ... is remarkable for

Table 4.3:   The patient and carer experience*

Experience of discharge	Percentage of patients	Percentage of carers
Patient was unready for discharge	19.7	30.8
Received less than 24 hours' notice of discharge	31.3	–
Would like more notice of discharge	16.1	30.8
Consulted about discharge plans	21	17.9
Patient given no information in hospital on any topic in preparation for discharge	47.7	–
Carer felt inadequately informed of patient's treatment and condition	–	44.6%
Readmitted to hospital within three months	27.7	–

*Adapted from Tierney *et al.* 1994b, pp. 37–38.

> the consistency of its findings. Problems of communication, coordination and information transfer have been routinely identified. Thus different professionals within a hospital may adopt different approaches to the timing and the process of discharge; communication between hospitals and primary care is often weak; and overlying these problems are differences in priorities, organisation and culture between health and local authorities.

Having reviewed the substantial literature that exists in this field, the King's Fund report identified three key themes:

1 Some groups, in particular older people, are sometimes discharged home without adequate preparation or without suitable arrangements in place in the community.
2 Delayed discharges result in an inappropriate or inefficient use of acute hospital beds. With pressures on acute care rising, this can lead to premature discharge for some patients.
3 There is a general lack of communication and co-ordination between hospital and community, and between health and social services.

Next, the King's Fund considered the impact of the 1989 government circular on hospital discharge. On the positive side, the circular emphasised the need for hospital doctors to be satisfied that adequate arrangements had been made for ongoing support in the community, the centrality of the patient and the key role of nursing staff. Despite this, however, the circular is criticised for:

- focusing more on professional accountability than on the process of discharge planning
- neglecting the complexity of hospital discharge
- failing to discuss the tension between maintaining a rapid throughput of patients with the needs of patients or carers

- supplying insufficient detail on the transfer of responsibility between hospital and community services
- a lack of clarity regarding responsibility for monitoring discharge policies at a local level
- a lack of national monitoring to identify the overall picture of discharge policy, successful initiatives or difficulties in implementing the circular
- failing to translate policy into practice – there is evidence to suggest that implementation of the circular is patchy.

Above all, however, the King's Fund report was critical of a much more general failure to consider hospital discharge as a discrete area for management concern and policy or professional development. This contrasts with other healthcare systems (such as in the USA), where the need for insurance companies to reimburse hospitals for the care provided has led to a greater emphasis on ensuring that people are appropriately admitted to hospital, stay for an appropriate length of time and are successfully discharged. Overall, the report concluded that hospital discharge is a complex process, perhaps requiring greater central intervention, and that there is some way to go before we achieve the goal of seamless care (Marks 1994, p. 6):

> By definition, discharge spans organisational and professional boundaries. While managerial changes within any organisation can address some of the problems identified, management fiat is by no means an adequate response. [This report] identifies areas of policy uncertainty, where joint approaches, sensitive to local options and individual circumstances, are required. Even here, however, conflicts between national policy and local opportunities can muddy the discharge process. It is therefore important to debate and clarify at national policy level rights of access to post-discharge care, and not to cast such fundamental questions as local management issues. The implementation of the NHS and Community Care Act makes it a matter of urgency that these issues are now resolved.

Also in 1994, an episode of the television programme, *Panorama*, sought to address the issue of hospital discharge and changes in the boundary between health and social care (BBC 1994). Beginning with a speech by the then Prime Minister, John Major, the programme sought to demonstrate how many older people were facing what he described as 'the greatest nightmare': being 'old, sick, poor and uncared for'. Drawing on interviews with users, carers, practitioners and politicians, the show focused on a series of case studies to highlight how inappropriate or premature hospital discharge and debates between health and social service managers about who should fund different types of care were affecting the lives of ordinary people. Although some may feel that the programme had a particular argument to put across and was sometimes far from dispassionate, the images and stories it contained were a powerful indictment of current discharge policy and practice (*see* Box 4.3).

Box 4.3 The greatest nightmare

Two district nurses visited an 88-year-old man who had been sitting in his chair all night unable to move. The waste bin beside him was full of urine and cigarette butts, and the man was unable to walk or reach a toilet. He had recently been discharged from hospital, although the first people to be told of his discharge were not the district nurses but the man's neighbours, via a message left on their answerphone. In a bag of dirty washing brought home from hospital, the nurse found a letter stating that the patient had been referred to social services for home care and meals-on-wheels. Despite this, these services did not turn up for four days. As the man was readmitted to hospital, a voice-over observed how 'this attempt at community care seems to have been a spectacular failure. [The man] is now trapped in a revolving door between hospital and home'. According to a GP interviewed on the programme, 'the situation ... worries me hugely. I hear you have someone who's really frail, elderly and unwell being admitted, re-admitted and readmitted again to hospital. It's hugely damaging to his health emotionally and physically, and I know only too well how that can end up.'

One woman aged 90 spent the last two months of her life in and out of hospital. On her last discharge, her family felt that she was too ill to leave hospital, but ward staff allegedly put the phone down on them as they tried to voice their concerns.

A 77-year-old man with a brain tumour was paralysed down one side and lost his vision in one eye. The local hospice was full and his family was told to find a nursing home for him. They felt he was too ill to move, but doctors told them his condition was stable. This was contradicted by the man's medical notes which suggested that he was 'slowly deteriorating'. The man later died while the family were out looking at nursing homes.

A man with Alzheimer's disease was entirely dependent on others for his care and became the subject of a disagreement between the local health and social services as to who should fund his care. To resolve the issue, the man was observed over a three-day period and essentially 'carved up'. Since two hours and 40 minutes of each day were felt to be taken up with nursing tasks, the NHS was responsible for 11% of the bill for his care. This was described as 'ludicrous' and 'laughable' by the man's wife, who had been fighting for NHS funding for almost two years. When asked to clarify the boundary between

continued opposite

health and social care in this particular case, the Health Secretary suggested that:

- the boundary should be decided locally
- support was available to advise on individual cases
- both health and social care had received a great deal more money
- the interface between the two services was generally working much better than in the past.

A man paralysed from the neck down was felt to be 'blocking' a bed needed for more urgent cases and was about to be discharged. The consultant felt he was stable and that there was no scope for further medical intervention. When asked why the NHS would not pay for the man's care, the consultant looked embarrassed and suggested that the interviewer spoke to the health authority.

A man discharged from hospital in the evening received no help to get to bed and was unable to get out of his chair. His GP did not hear of his patient's discharge for two days. Despite the GP requesting social services assistance in helping the man to wash, no one came and the man had not had a bath for nearly one month.

Overall, the *Panorama* programme concluded that 'with the health service rewriting its promise to care and local authorities left to pick up the pieces, too many old people are being left with little or nothing'.

Source: BBC 1994

In 1995, the results of a research study carried out in south Wales were published in a collection of contributions on community care (Jones and Lester 1995). Based on postal questionnaires completed by a sample of 960 older people who had been discharged from hospital in the previous three months, the study asked about the older people's experiences of hospital care, discharge and after-care. Of the 960 people who returned their questionnaires, just over a third did not recall discussing their discharge with anyone, and hospital staff visited patients' homes to assess the suitability of the home environment in only 52 cases. Many patients also felt that they had inadequate notice of discharge (*see* Table 4.4) and some suggested that they had been discharged too soon with insufficient notice for carers to make the arrangements necessary for discharge (Jones and Lester 1995, p. 92):

They just told me I was going out and put me in an ambulance. (Female aged 93)

They tried to discharge him too soon, without fully explaining how to use the stoma bag. (Wife of male aged 78)

For those patients who returned directly home from hospital, most saw their spouse, family and friends as their principal source of support, and only a small minority (7%) named a statutory service as their main source of help. Some participants experienced difficulties in having services which they received prior to hospital admission reinstated on discharge, and others encountered problems coping at home with help not always provided.

Table 4.4: Notice of hospital discharge*

Notice of discharge	Percentage of patients (n = 960)
Informed of discharge on same day	33
Informed after visiting time the night before	16
Informed during previous evening's visiting time	23
Up to three days' notice	21
More than three days' notice	5

*Adapted from Jones and Lester 1995, p. 92.

Also in 1995, the SSI published the findings of inspections of the arrangements for discharging older people from hospital to residential or nursing care in seven SSDs (Department of Health/SSI 1995). With fieldwork carried out between October 1993 and March 1994, the inspectors were aware that their work was providing an early insight into the impact of the community care reforms (Department of Health/SSI 1995, p. 7):

> The importance attached to ensuring the effective implementation of assessment procedures within hospitals stemmed in part from a recognition that the new arrangements provided a 'litmus test' of the ability of social services and health agencies to work together more effectively. In particular, this was because of the potential impact on hospital resources of delays in discharge of older patients from hospital when residential or nursing home placements were required. The tensions between patient throughput and comprehensive assessment, and therefore between health and social care agencies, were potentially at their most acute.

Whilst all the local and health authorities concerned had developed hospital discharge agreements as required by the government (*see* Chapter 2) and although collaboration had improved, there was evidence of ongoing difficulties in some areas. Sometimes, the emphasis was on establishing the correct processes for hospital discharge without necessarily focusing on practice issues or ensuring that the process was responsive to the needs of users and carers. Progress was also patchy, so that some agencies had developed agreements through extensive consultation with practitioners, users and carers, invested heavily in training and developed robust mechanisms to monitor performance, whereas others had chosen to impose discharge procedures from above without adequate training for staff or satisfactory monitoring arrangements. Involving hospital doctors and GPs in training could also be problematic (Department of Health/SSI 1995, p. 12):

> In many authorities there were concerns about consultants either pre-judging the outcome of assessments or pressurising for discharge. In one authority users had reportedly been transported to residential care and nursing homes after 9.00 pm and sometimes discharged precipitously and against social work advice. In another SSD staff reported that there was continuous pressure from consultants to discharge patients before they were ready. One vulnerable older person was reported to have been discharged without the knowledge of the social worker.

In addition the SSI inspection raised a number of other issues.

- The provision of information was found to be very ad hoc with no evidence of a coherent and resourced approach. Information was particularly lacking for people who did not speak English or those with sensory impairments, and there was little written information to help users and carers make important choices about residential and nursing care.
- Referral mechanisms varied widely, with some referrals coming by word of mouth and being prioritised by individual social workers with little management supervision. Many hospital social work teams were dealing with a significant increase in the volume of referrals and there was confusion among some ward staff as to the most appropriate time to refer patients for SSD assistance.
- In some areas, hospital staff were pre-judging the outcome of assessments and referring people for services, such as residential and nursing care, before social work assessments were completed.
- Many hospital workers felt that they were not kept informed as to how assessments were progressing.
- Some care planning was entirely verbal, with no written documentation. Some residential and nursing homes did not receive adequate information about the needs of people discharged straight from hospital, and only one SSD shared written care plans with users and carers.
- Financial assessments could sometimes be problematic due to a lack of training, poor information for users or carers and a shortage of finance staff.
- There was very little information to help service users choose which home to enter and very few users visited homes before placement.
- Some patients had to wait for long periods for hospital transport or were discharged at inappropriate times (such as late at night).

Also in 1995, the *Health Service Journal* published an article based on hospital discharge guidance drawn up by older people from an innovative and highly publicised project to involve frail older people from Fife in decisions about their health and social care (Barnes *et al.* 1994; Barnes and Bennett 1998; Barnes and Bennett-Emslie 1997; Cormie 1999). The Fife User Panels each contained between six and eight frail older people and sought to enable older people unable to get out of the house without support to meet together to express their needs and their experiences of services. In the process, the Fife initiative had to respond to significant practical difficulties – arranging transport to and from meetings, providing accessible venues, encouraging participants to express their views and overcoming deaths, hospital admissions and entry into residential care. Despite this, an evaluation of the User Panels suggested that the project enabled participants to learn from each other, enhanced self-esteem and provided valued social contact (Barnes and Bennett-Emslie 1997). In addition, the Panels were also felt to have had an impact on some services and were generally well-received by service providers. However, perhaps the most crucial aspect of the Fife initiative was its attempt to involve a user group often excluded from service planning as a result of assumptions made about the capacity of older people to participate in decisions about their care and about service delivery more generally. As Marian Barnes (1997, p. 64) observes, 'the particular significance of this project is that it seeks to support collective organisation among people often assumed to be too old, frail or tired to meet together with the objective of seeking change'.

Although the Fife User Panels have been described in much more detail elsewhere, a key outcome from the project was a good practice guide to hospital discharge (Barnes and Cormie 1995). With personal experience of admission to and discharge from hospital, panel members identified a range of problems with current practice (*see* Box 4.4)

Box 4.4 On the panel

Members of the Fife User Panels project recounted their personal experiences of hospital discharge:

- Being given no advance warning and being told during a relative's visit that they could go home immediately.
- Being packed and ready to go but having to wait hours until an ambulance service was available.
- Returning to cold and empty houses with no services available until the following day.

One panel member found she was expected to provide help for an elderly neighbour who was returned home with no support. There had been no discussion with her; it was simply assumed that she would look after her neighbour.

Source: Barnes and Cormie 1995, pp. 30–31

To overcome these issues, panel members recommended a 14-point plan for good hospital discharge, which was subsequently adopted by local service providers (Fife User Panels Project 1994 (emphasis in the original); *see also* Barnes and Cormie 1995; Fife Council Home Care Service n.d.):

- The heating should be turned on in the house from the morning of discharge. The bed should be made up and **warm** for the patient.
- There should be fresh staple goods (such as milk, tea, eggs and butter) in the house.
- One meal should be ready for the person coming home.
- The home carer should be in the house awaiting the patient's arrival if no friends or relatives are available or if requested by the patient.
- Adequate notice of discharge should be given to family members (remembering that this person in turn will have to make their own domestic arrangements).
- Discharge times should be given within reasonable parameters (for example, whether discharge will take place in the morning, afternoon or early evening). People should not be kept waiting for hours.
- At least 24–48 hours notice of discharge should be given.
- Services should be in place **on the day** of discharge, not the day after.
- Services following discharge should be available for seven days per week, including public holidays.
- The GP should call on the day of discharge to make sure the patient is settled.
- Nurses should tuck the person down at night at a reasonable time for the patient. This service should continue until both parties agree that it is no longer required.
- Arrangements should be made for keys to be given to carers to allow them into the person's home before the person comes out of hospital.
- It should be ensured that on discharge there is a carer who has willingly accepted and is physically capable of undertaking the caring role.
- Someone at the hospital should make all the necessary arrangements. Panel members regretted the passing of the hospital almoner, who had previously performed this role.

For all this to happen, panel members also emphasised the need for:

- good links between nurses or hospital staff, the social work department and others who are part of the community care package, as well as family and neighbours a few weeks **in advance** of discharge
- **monitoring** of discharges to make sure that services that should be in place are, and that they are working smoothly to the patient's satisfaction.

In 1996, the results of a study funded by the Joseph Rowntree Foundation into the experiences of older people going through the process of hospital discharge were published (Clark *et al.* 1996). Working in two hospital trusts in southern England, the researchers conducted in-depth interviews with approximately 50 older people who had been assessed by hospital occupational therapists (OTs) and issued with equipment and/or had their homes adapted. From the beginning, the study highlighted the incompatibility of the need to secure a speedy discharge from acute care with the emphasis of the community care reforms on promoting independence (*see* Box 4.5). In one case, an older person had been readmitted to hospital on several occasions. At each discharge, the hospital contacted the local home care manager directly to reinstate the person's home care package, rather than go through the more lengthy process of making a referral to a social worker. Although this may have enabled the patient in question to be discharged as quickly as possible, it also meant that the individual's care package was not reviewed and that she did not have an allocated social worker. Elsewhere in the study, the researchers highlighted the lack of formal feedback from social services in one of the study areas, resulting in a situation where hospital OTs do not know what happens to patients after discharge and cannot evaluate the effectiveness of their intervention. This had been overcome to a certain extent in the second case study site, via an OT appointed to follow up patients in the community, and by use of a booklet listing the names and numbers of each person the patient has had contact with whilst in hospital. In addition to the competing pressures faced by OTs, the study also shed light on the experiences of individual older people. From the perspective of the patient, hospital discharges may be viewed as something over which the individual has little control, with the professionals deciding when people are 'allowed' to go home. Some older people are also bewildered by the range of people they have encountered while in hospital and are not sure precisely who they have seen or which professional is responsible for which aspect of their care.

Box 4.5   Promoting independence versus swift discharge

The demands on hospital OTs involved in discharge planning and assessment are such that for those working in acute wards, there is little or no time for them to try to maximise the individual's functioning through the use of remedial therapy to improve mobility, dexterity and confidence ... Hospital OTs working in slow-stream wards and rehabilitation wards have the opportunity to practise more ongoing remedial therapy with patients and to try out different forms of equipment to find out which best suits their particular needs. In acute wards, however, OT input is more episodic and the service offered is discharge facilitation. The agenda for safe discharge is different from the rehabilitation agenda.

continued opposite

The primary focus of hospital OTs involved in discharge planning is on the functional capacities of patients in terms of the basic activities of daily living. This means a focus predominantly on personal care activities and domestic activities, such as cooking, housework, bed-making/changing, laundry and shopping. OTs sometimes express their frustration about this: they would like to adopt a more holistic approach, taking into account wider personal and social needs, but they are constrained by limited time and staffing resources and therefore have to concentrate upon the 'basics' to get the patient home safely.

Initially the research project had hoped to look at the impact and experience of having major ... housing adaptations, but in fact we came across very few such cases in the context of discharge from acute ward settings ... [One possible explanation is that] major housing adaptations are ways of answering long-term needs and this doesn't gel with the short-term nature of the solutions demanded by the throughput of patients from acute settings ... As one senior hospital OT put it: 'Basically, when you've got two days to discharge you start to do the priority things, which is getting that person home safely.'

There is an assumption, echoed in policy documents, that assessment is comprehensive and systematic. In reality, in the context of hospital discharge, assessments are conducted in a very small snapshot in time.
Source: Clark *et al.* 1996, pp. 14, 17–18, 33 and 57

Also in 1996, the *Health Service Journal* published the results of a joint initiative undertaken by Birmingham Social Services and Birmingham Heartlands Hospital Trust with a view to improving their understanding of hospital discharge (Roberts and Houghton 1996). This project had originally arisen out of apparently heated debates about who was to blame for delayed discharges (Roberts and Houghton 1996, p. 28):

> This time last year [i.e. winter 1995] acute hospitals in Birmingham were under severe pressure. A high number of bed days were being lost because of delays in patient discharge. This led to unacceptable delays in admission, with patients waiting many hours for a bed and adverse media attention. The trusts blamed the local social services department. This was not surprising given the widespread view within the NHS that social services are the main cause of bed-blocking because they do not meet assessment and care planning timescales or do not have funding for services. The social services department argued that the existing format for collecting data on delays did not have enough detail, and so was open to mis-interpretation. Following heated exchanges, it was agreed that a constructive investigation was needed to find out what was really happening on the wards.

In response to this situation, local health and social care organisations sought to develop more accurate methods of data collection which would be acceptable to all parties. Having redesigned the hospital's bed occupancy data collection form, the partners conducted a full survey of Heartlands Hospital in March 1996, and appear to have been surprised by the findings of this process. Contrary to popular opinion, the vast majority of delays were attributable neither to the SSD or to the hospital, but were the result of factors beyond the control of either agency (*see* Table 4.5). This led the researchers to conclude that so-called 'bed-blocking' is much more complex than it may at first appear and that a joint approach to data collection and to tackling delayed discharges is required (Roberts and Houghton 1996, p. 29):

> This pilot project disproved the simple theory that social services are to blame for bed-blocking. For this joint approach to work elsewhere, managers at all levels both within acute trusts and social services will need to work hard at understanding each other's culture, policies and procedures, agree robust criteria and mechanisms for monitoring delays, and make a commitment to take action either as an individual agency or jointly to resolve issues that have been identified.

Table 4.5:   Who's to blame?*

Reason for delay	Total patients	Total days of delay
Trust responsible for delay		
Awaiting geriatric bed within the hospital trust	4	51
MRSA delaying discharge	2	54
Awaiting OT assessment	4	32
Awaiting OT home visits	1	7
Awaiting opinion of consultant	5	29
Subtotal	16	173
SSD responsible for delay		
Comprehensive assessment by social worker	3	41
Awaiting funding authorisation for nursing home	2	16
Awaiting home equipment	1	6
Awaiting home care	4	17
Subtotal	10	80
Delays beyond the control of either agency		
Awaiting bed in other NHS hospital	3	42
Patient or carer-led reasons	15	2800
Community health services	3	71
Community health services and social services (joint)	1	7
Awaiting residential vacancy	2	21
Awaiting nursing home vacancy	4	72
Awaiting rehousing (private housing)	1	8
(local authority)	2	26
Lack of long-term healthcare provision	1	156
Subtotal	32	3203
Total	58	3456

*Adapted from Roberts and Houghton 1996, p. 28.

In the same year, researchers at the Nuffield Institute for Health published the findings of their research into hospital discharge and the perspectives of service users, carers and professionals (Godfrey and Moore 1996). Based on qualitative research with individuals from six Leeds hospital wards, the study identified a discrepancy between the perceptions of staff and users or carers as to the extent to which the latter were involved in assessment and care planning, with carers in particular feeling that communication between the hospital and themselves had been inadequate. Often, 'users and carers tended not to be aware of there being any ongoing process of assessing their needs or planning for their discharge. Most felt that any planning that did take place only began a few days before they actually left the hospital' (Godfrey and Moore 1996, p. 49). Although most users and their carers expressed satisfaction with the care they received, there was a range of isolated difficulties, such as a premature discharge, a lack of clarity about the purpose of medication and delays in hospital transport. On discharge, some patients found that items of equipment they had been promised did not materialise and there were concerns about evening or night time services, bathing services, the difficulty in giving routine medicine to people living alone and communication between hospital and community services (*see* Box 4.6). Those discharged to a residential or nursing home tended not to have much choice over where they went, with discharge dependent upon a place being available. Whilst managers and staff felt that they understood policy and procedure with regard to community care and hospital discharge, such understanding was not always translated into practice in situations where this would involve challenging previous ways of working. Examples included difficulties in working across the hospital–community boundary and shifting the traditional patient–professional relationship in order to involve patients and carers in decisions about treatment and discharge.

Box 4.6 Hospital discharge: the perspectives of users, carers and professionals

One woman, discharged on a Friday and readmitted the following Monday, felt she had been discharged too soon: 'The first time no, I didn't feel ready. They sent me home and I didn't refuse. I still felt poorly. They must have felt I was alright. I didn't fell well enough to come home.'

Some users were not sure as to the purpose of their medication: 'Ever since, I've had some little tiny pills which I presume were for my heart, so I don't know whether they are or not.'

continued overleaf

Some people experienced long delays waiting for an ambulance without receiving an explanation or any reassurance: 'The doctor told me I was going home in the morning. It got to dinner time and there was no sign of anybody coming to fetch me. I thought they'd forgotten about me.'

On a number of occasions, items of equipment that had been promised did not materialise or were inappropriate: 'The hospital gave her the zimmer but I've had to change it though. It was far too big.'

One person felt that they received an inadequate amount of care on returning home: 'I think I could have had more support than what I've had and I think that one hour a fortnight for cleaning is just ridiculous. The night carers came to help me to bed, but because I got a little independent she stopped them altogether. I think it's stopped too soon … I think I've been victimised with trying to be a little bit independent. It just stopped dead.'

Some people experienced a lack of communication over service provision: 'The first time my mother came home I'd arranged for people to put her to bed because she was a bit frightened. But they didn't come so she sat up all night. I rang home care the next day and they said they'd had a letter from the hospital to say she hadn't come home. [After a second discharge] home care said they'd sort out for someone to come at night. But when I rang home care to let them know it was definite she was coming out of hospital, I was told they had rung the hospital and had been informed that the home care service wasn't really needed; my mother could get in and out of bed as she'd been doing it in the hospital. So I had a word with the sister on the ward on the morning I went to pick my mother up. She said she'd no idea who home care had spoken to, but that it was a very good idea for them to be involved.'

Source: Godfrey and Moore 1996, pp. 50–52, 59–61

In 1997, a government circular published details of monitoring carried out on the implementation of the 1995 hospital discharge/continuing care guidance, HSG(95)8/LAC(95)5. In an annex to the circular, the Department of Health included a specific reference to findings with regard to the causes of delayed hospital discharges (Department of Health 1997c):

As part of their review of eligibility criteria policy [for continuing care] most [health authorities], in partnership with the [local authority], have also reviewed their hospital discharge arrangements and protocols. This year has seen a move away from the 'blame' culture between the two agencies. Many have taken a whole system approach to analysing how their discharge procedures work particularly in response to difficulties over delayed discharges. Some of the causes of delayed discharge remain with health – access to continuing care beds, awaiting specialist clinical opinion, unrealistic discharge dates. Some are due to social services – no available finance for placements/packages, lengthy timescales for assessment, inadequate levels of hospital social work. Some are beyond the control of both agencies – lack of suitable residential or nursing homes, patient/family/carer choice of care. Some causes have been the lack of appropriate services which [health and local authorities] are now beginning to develop – hospital at home, rehabilitation teams in the community, intensive aftercare services, investment in specialist equipment. There remains a need to manage the market to change the independent sector provision and reconfigure the in-house services and current contracts to provide alternatives to hospital admission.

Finally, 1997 also saw the publication of Henwood *et al.*'s (1997) study of hospital discharge arrangements in six localities. Building on previous research in this area (Henwood and Wistow 1993) and taking place as part of a wider study into inter-agency collaboration, the researchers found that considerable progress had been made in clarifying roles and responsi-bilities between health and social care agencies at a local level. Often, this local activity was driven at least in part by the central policy agenda, and government requirements in preparing for and implementing the com-munity care reforms (*see* Chapter 3) were found to have been helpful in focusing attention on long-standing issues. However, the study also found evidence of a number of difficulties, including:

- difficulties implementing agreed hospital discharge procedures in prac-tice compared to apparent success in reaching local policy agreement
- a lack of consistency between specialties
- different notions of good practice held by health and social care
- inadequate communication and information
- difficulties engaging GPs and primary healthcare in hospital discharge
- resource pressures
- the need to develop a more strategic approach to hospital discharge by recognising the interdependence of admission, rehabilitation/recovery and discharge.

Overall, the researchers concluded that (Henwood *et al.* 1997, p. ii):

Hospital discharge was ... a matter of continuing difficulty in all of the six localities. The implementation of agreed arrangements for hospital discharge was acknowledged to be patchy, and there were particular difficulties in securing consistency across the various specialties. There were recognised deficiencies in communication and coordination within and between agencies. The issue of 'blocked beds' was one of recurrent concern in all localities. The identification of problems with blocked beds is often the result of an over-simplified analysis of discharge practice, and it is apparent that many factors in relation both to admission, treatment and discharge, can all contribute to the emergence of diffi-culties. Social services and healthcare providers face inherent difficulties in their interaction because of often conflicting perspectives on the pace at which discharges can be accomplished. The issue of blocked beds can often be seen as a particular indicator of the general state of working relations between health and social services ... and is more often associated with attempts to attribute blame to other parties than to establish operational solutions to problems.

Research findings II

Following on from the review of recent research findings, Chapter 5 focuses on research during New Labour's time in office since the 1997 general election. After this, a concluding section considers the experience of user groups other than older people and of Northern Ireland, Scotland and Wales.

In 1998, the SSI published the results of an inspection into hospital discharge arrangements in eight local authorities (Horne 1998). Although discharge practice and joint working more generally were 'getting better', the inspectorate felt that there was still some way to go (Horne 1998, pp. 1–3):

> Older people today are discharged from hospital, and living in the community, with higher levels of dependency and greater or more 'complex' health and social care needs ... However, it has not been uncommon for health and social services to hold differing perspectives about where the responsibility of provision lies. In some cases social services have viewed themselves as victims of cost-shunting from health services, and health agencies have blamed social services' cost cutting and changes in eligibility criteria for delays in placing people awaiting discharge from hospital ... Overall, hospital discharge arrangements are getting better in some important areas, although much remains to be done. Users and carers were satisfied with the services they received and users were typically involved in assessment and care planning processes. At the operational level hospital based staff were working well together, usually responding promptly to referrals and were able to resolve most cross organisational issues before they impacted directly on users or escalated into formal complaints. Co-ordination and communication with community based health or social services staff, however, remained limited ... [Despite progress in many areas] the distribution of care plans, the completion of reviews and the inconsistency of initial screening continues to cause concern. Some authorities had reached joint agreements and some had developed rehabili-tative services but considerable scope for improvement remained. Monitoring information and performance measures were not robust enough to allow managers in social services or across agencies to chart service development effectively.

Other areas of concern included:

- Delays in the provision of adaptations to users' homes or the provision of more appropriate housing. This was the result of factors such as a short-age of OTs, inadequate resources to meet demands and insufficiently early involvement of housing departments in the discharge planning process.
- A lack of assessments of the needs of carers.

- A lack of clarity about the best time to refer patients to SSDs.
- A tendency in one area to delay 'simple' assessments until after patients had returned home, thereby introducing inappropriate delays in service provision and potentially jeopardising the success of the discharge in question.
- A lack of genuinely multi-disciplinary assessments in some areas.
- A lack of inputs by community-based staff.
- Service-led rather than needs-led assessments.
- A failure to review care plans in more than half the cases inspected.
- In some areas, a history of mistrust and mutual recrimination made successful joint working more complex.

About the same time as the SSI reported on hospital discharge arrangements, the Scottish Office Central Research Unit published the results of its review of the literature on the discharge of frail older people (Taraborrelli *et al.* 1998). Based on a review of networked library services, CD-Rom databases and visits to selected libraries and documentation centres, with case studies of discharge practice at four Scottish hospital trusts, the report provided a detailed overview of the discharge process (*see* Box 5.1 for an overview of the key findings).

Box 5.1　The hospital discharge of frail older people

- The roots of inappropriate bed use and delayed discharge often lie in the process of admission.
- Admission protocols need to provide for the screening of patients requiring community care assessment and possible referral to other agencies. Screening is particularly important to ensure that social work assessments of community care needs are not automatically requested but are targeted on the most appropriate users.
- Assessment for discharge varies greatly in extensiveness and in multi-disciplinarity.
- Appropriate discharge requires a period of preparation, adequate notice of discharge to appropriate parties, discussion of after-care arrangements with users and/or carers, liaison with community care professionals, education of users and/or carers (e.g. in respect of medication), a comprehensive and effective system of information collection and dissemination between the hospital and community, and co-ordination by a skilled and knowledgeable 'named nurse'.
- Liaison between community and hospital continues to cause problems. Associated with liaison difficulties are reported tensions and clashes of perspectives, rooted in the management of competing priorities and in different budgets.

continued opposite

- Joint/shared documentation in discharge planning is still not universal and is little evaluated. There is only patchy in-patient documentation of users' social circumstances and informal care arrangements. Only limited use is made of validated scales to assess functional and mental capacities.
- Discharge liaison nurses are reported to facilitate earlier discharge, improve after-care and reduce readmission rates but can only be a partial solution to the complexities of hospital discharge.
- Professionally-led supported discharge schemes are thought to be highly cost-effective. Voluntary-sector discharge schemes (using both paid and volunteer staff) are thought to be a valuable complement to statutory provision, but not a replacement for such provision; sometimes such schemes were inadequately geared into GP services and the work of nurses and home helps.
- GPs value receiving direct and informative discharge summaries on the same day as their patient's discharge.

Source: Taraborrelli *et al.* 1998, pp. i–iii

In four case study hospital trusts, there was evidence of a number of problems:

- Funding constraints, particularly on social work budgets.
- Professional relationships between health and social services and practical restrictions on multi-disciplinary working.
- Difficulties in monitoring successful implementation of discharge procedures.
- Limited involvement of GPs and, still more, of housing officers, nursing home officers, and the voluntary sector in discharge planning.
- Duplication of effort, particularly with regard to assessments.
- A limited formal commitment in official documentation to involvement of patients and their relatives in discharge planning.

Source: Taraborrelli *et al.* 1998, pp. i–iii

Also in 1998, the Carers National Association (now Carers UK) published the results of a study looking at approximately 3000 carers' experiences of the NHS (Henwood 1998). Just over a third of respondents said that the person they cared for had been admitted to hospital in the last 12 months. Although many felt that the hospital stay as a whole had been well-organised, they reported a range of concerns about the discharge process (*see* Table 5.1 and Box 5.2). Key themes included a failure to involve carers in discharge planning or to discuss options other than continuing to care for the person being discharged. In particular, many carers felt that the person they cared for was discharged from hospital too soon and that inadequate after-care arrangements left carers having to cope with extremely difficult situations (*see* Box 5.2) (Henwood 1998, pp. 33 and 39):

> The length of time which people spend in hospital has been getting shorter, and hospitals are under constant pressure to maintain 'throughput' and treat as many people as possible in order to reduce waiting lists and meet efficiency targets. One consequence of this is that some people may be discharged before they are ready. One in four of the carers in the survey felt that the person they cared for had not been discharged at the right time, and in more than 80% of these cases, carers believed that discharge had taken place too soon. One in four of the people who had been treated as in-patients were re-admitted to hospital within two months … It is, at the very least, a possibility that some of these re-admissions were of people discharged too soon whose deterioration required further hospital care. Discharging people too soon is not cost-effective, and too much attention to speed rather than quality of discharge is likely to prove shortsighted. While there may be savings to hospitals, there will also be costs in the form of unplanned re-admissions. There will also be costs to other parts of the health and social care system which have to respond to increased needs in the community, but most significantly there are likely to be considerable costs (including stress and ill health) falling on patients and their carers.

> Despite the recognition by the Department of Health of the vital importance of good hospital discharge arrangements, the experiences of respondents indicate that poor discharges are still prevalent, with carers too often left to cope with inadequate information, and insufficient support.

Table 5.1: Carers' views of hospital discharge*

Experience of discharge	*Percentage of carers*
Consulted over discharge plans	71
Carers' concerns taken into account	62
Helped to prepare for discharge	54
Told about care needs of person being cared for	48
Told about options other than continuing to care for the person at home	28
Given copy of discharge plan	25
Person not discharged at the right time	25
Person being cared for readmitted to hospital within two months	25

*Adapted from Henwood 1998, pp. 32–35.

Box 5.2   Carers and hospital discharge

'I was told that my wife could transfer (e.g. move herself from bed to chair) very well. Then they discharged her. After that I found out it took three people to transfer her in [hospital]. She came home to me, and only me. It was left to me alone to transfer her to the toilet and bed, feed and wash her … is this care in the community?'

'I visited her each day in hospital, and was informed that she was fit enough to be brought home by ambulance … The hospital was well aware that I was her sole carer, as I watched the nurse write all this information down on her arrival. I suffer from lower back pain, and this was made much worse by having to lift my mother to a sitting position while in bed, and twisting round with her to help her onto her commode, then lifting her back into bed, as I found very quickly she had no strength to lift herself up at all, following her discharge from hospital. As well as caring for her every need during the day, I found I had to get up during the night to attend to her toilet require-ments. The night after her discharge she fell out of bed, and I had to dial 999 as it was impossible for me to lift her.'

Old people seem to be discharged from hospital too soon after treat-ment or operations. The majority of carers are not medically qualified. Post-operative care for older people should be in the hospital where they received their treatment. It is not fair or correct to expect carers to carry out post-operative care which in my case was devastating.
Source: quoted in Henwood 1998, pp. 34–35

In 1999, researchers in the north-east of England published the results of a study into the nursing implications of older people discharged from hos-pital to care homes (Reed and Morgan 1999). Whilst there is a substantial literature on hospital discharge and older people, the authors observe that most commentators focus on discharge from acute care to patients' own homes, overlooking those patients who are not able to return home and who have to enter residential or nursing care. Although this may involve less nursing input to organise and co-ordinate care, the authors argue that discharge to a care home frequently involves a transfer from the public to the independent sector and from health to social care, and is therefore potentially extremely complex. Based on interviews with older people or family members, and on focus groups with health and social care staff, the study found that many of the older people were extremely passive in the discharge process. In particular, many participants seemed prepared to accept the view of staff that it was time to leave hospital, did not challenge staff perceptions that they should enter residential or nursing care and exercised very little choice over which home they entered. For family members, the process of choosing a home on their relative's behalf could be complex and sometimes had to be conducted in a rushed manner due to time constraints imposed by the hospital. In terms of health and social care practitioners, hospital nurses tended not to discuss older people's forthcoming discharge to a care home unless the older person initiated the conversation and felt that they did not know enough about residential or nursing care to support patients. Some were also hostile to the independent sector and were reluctant to collaborate with care home staff. In contrast, social workers had much more contact with residential or nursing care homes, yet felt disempowered by the discharge process (*see* Box 5.3). Medical staff felt that it was not part of their role to provide support for older people moving into a care home and were concerned about delays caused by the lack of social services funding (*see* Box 5.3). Overall, the researchers concluded that (Reed and Morgan 1999, p. 825):

> there is some confusion between nursing staff, medical staff and social workers about who is responsible for which aspects of the discharge procedure, with each professional group assuming that another has chief responsibility or input. For the future development of discharge processes, multidisciplinary teams need to clarify what responsibilities each group has, and ensure that contact with older people is documented to reflect this.

In addition, the authors felt that nursing staff could offer much greater support to older people leaving hospital for a care home by:

- being proactive in initiating discussions about the transition from hospital to care homes
- learning more about the care home setting
- reflecting on their assumptions about the independent sector
- supporting older people to exercise choice and express preferences.

Box 5.3 Social work versus medical perspectives

Social work perspectives:

Social workers had more contact with care homes, and more knowledge of the systems of regulation and funding care, but this expertise did not necessarily give them a feeling of control over the process. They felt that they were responding primarily to pressures from medical staff to organize discharges and did not have time to spend with patients discussing their choices and preferences. They talked about their professional skills in providing support as being eroded by

continued opposite

their administrative role in processing assessments and arrangements for care. One social worker described her role as being driven by these demands:

'I don't spend the time I used to – it's just you get a message from the medical staff – this one's to go out, and you just sort out the paper-work and maybe talk to the family. Sometimes I don't even get to see the client.'

Medical perspectives:

Medical staff, however, felt that their role was mainly in making discharge decisions and deciding the level of care required from a medical point of view. Their concern was that the move was made quickly. And that it was not governed by Social Services Department financial considerations. They talked of their concern with patients who were waiting to come into hospital, which had to over-ride their concern with those who had received treatment and who had no fur-ther need of acute care.

Source: Reed and Morgan 1999, p. 824

Also in 1999, Help the Aged published background information on the NHS and the care of older people in hospital as part of its Dignity on the Ward campaign (Festing 1999). Summarising evidence from a number of recent research studies, the briefing made specific reference to problems associated with hospital discharge (Festing 1999, p. 11):

Although there were some excellent local initiatives, there was evidence of con-tinued problems with discharge planning and accessibility of effective alternative services in the community. Part of this stems from the problems of effective inter-agency working between health and social services. There were some good ini-tiatives in relation to rehabilitation programmes for older people, but the extent and range of these services – particularly in community settings to support people after discharge – was generally limited … There has been a marked reduction in the average length of stay in hospital for elderly people. Such an early discharge policy is more likely to benefit both the patients and the hospital service. How-ever, the success of early discharge depends on effective discharge planning and the availability of appropriate support in the weeks following discharge. Overall, hospital discharge arrangements are getting better in some important areas, although much remains to be done … Deficiencies in discharge planning have been identified in three main areas: communication between professionals, poor information provision to patients, and late or inadequate provision of community services.

Difficulties in securing co-ordinated hospital discharges were also identified in 1999 by the House of Commons Health Committee as part of its report on the relationship between health and social services (House of Commons Health Committee 1999, p. xviii):

> Effective liaison between health and social services is particularly important when patients are being discharged from hospital. As we have stated [elsewhere], users and carers often do not receive written discharge plans, and often do not appear to be involved in discussion about discharge arrangements. Nor, in many cases, do they believe that health and social services co-operate effectively over such arrangements; social services are not always involved in discharge planning from an early stage and once at home there are sometimes co-ordination problems.

Crucially, however, the Committee moved beyond simply highlighting the problematic nature of hospital discharge and sought to place this in the wider context of the contested boundary between health and social care (*see* Chapter 7 for further discussion). Thus, having described the problems experienced by users and carers, the Committee highlighted a series of structural barriers to working together (*see* Box 5.4). Drawing on a number of good practice examples and on the experience of the integrated services in place in Northern Ireland (*see below*), the Committee called for a new, unified health and social care system (House of Commons Health Committee 1999, p. xviii [emphasis in the original]):

> We consider the current system for continuing health and social care to be very confused. Responsibilities are blurred, professionals face unnecessary problems, and users and carers are suffering because of barriers created by a structural division which is based on an ill-defined and arguably non-existent boundary. We commend all those who have tried to establish seamless care for users and carers despite these barriers. They have shown levels of personal commitment and determination which we regard as admirable ... **However we consider that the problems of collaboration between health and social services will not be properly resolved until there is an integrated health and social care system, whether this is within the NHS, within local government or within some new, separate organisation. We acknowledge that such an integration would lead to an emphasis on the boundary between the health and social care body and other functions, for instance housing and education, but we believe that it is the only sensible long term solution to end the current confusion.**

Box 5.4 Barriers to working together

- Lack of clarity of role and responsibilities
- Financial barriers
- Different charging policies
- Legal barriers
- Different priorities
- Lack of coterminosity
- Different cultures
- Differences in democratic accountability
    Source: House of Commons Health Committee 1999, pp. xx–xxv

---

In 2000, the National Audit Office published a report on admissions and bed management in acute hospitals. Although the report focused on a wide range of issues, it did provide numerical data to illustrate the scope and implications of delayed hospital discharges (National Audit Office 2000, pp. 51–52):

- Delayed discharges were affecting nearly 6000 older people on any given day.
- Of 43 500 patients aged 75 and over occupying acute hospital beds in September 1999, 5550 (12.8%) were ready for discharge but delayed from leaving hospital.
- Almost all health authorities reported delays in discharging older patients, with the proportion of patients affected ranging from 1% to approximately 30% (with two health authorities reporting 61% and 81%). The latter figure was reported by Hillingdon Health Authority, where a very high proportion of patients were awaiting social services funding for residential or nursing home placements.
- 2.2 million bed days are lost each year as a result of delays in discharging older patients. This costs around £1 million per day.
- The causes of delayed discharge include internal factors (such as decisions to discharge being taken too late in the day for the patient to go home until the next day, delays in obtaining take-home medication and the availability of patient transport services) as well as external factors (*see* Table 5.2).

Table 5.2: The causes of delayed discharges*

Cause of delayed discharge	Percentage of NHS acute trusts reporting factor as a prime cause of delayed discharge
Internal factors	
Timing of consultant decision to discharge	52
Delays in take-home medicines	30
Delays in patient transport services	24
External factors	
Delays in social services assessment/funding	34
Lack of residential/nursing home places	31
Delays in provision of home care/equipment	21

*Adapted from National Audit Office 2000, pp. 53–55.

During its research, the National Audit Office found that 77% of NHS acute trusts have policies on patient discharge, although the report offers no comment on why this figure is not 100%. Although policies are circulated within the acute trusts, they are less widely agreed and circulated outside. Whilst many trusts plan discharge at the earliest opportunity and make early referrals to social services, not all do so and there is scope for improvement. A key figure in facilitating effective discharge was found to be the discharge (or care) co-ordinator, employed by 71% of trusts. Discharge lounges can also release hospital beds and are used by 58% of trusts, thereby freeing hospital beds for new admissions and providing a single collection point for patients leaving the hospital. However, these were not always used appropriately, since some wards were slow to transfer patients to the discharge lounge and since some staff felt that lounges added to their workload by removing relatively independent patients and allowing their beds to be filled by patients who are more acutely ill. Home support services enabling patients to receive health and social care at home were also found to facilitate swift discharge and are in operation in 40% of acute trusts. In seeking to improve discharge practices, the National Audit Office recommended that hospitals work in partnership with social services and community hospitals to co-ordinate the discharge process and summarised the essential features of an effective discharge policy (*see* Box 5.5).

Box 5.5   Good practice in discharging patients

The key features of an effective hospital discharge policy are that it:

- Is integrated within the local eligibility criteria for continuing care
- Covers the whole hospital and all patients discharged
- Establishes a protocol for management of patients whose discharge is delayed
- Is based on consultation with key interest groups within the hospital
- Is developed in consultation with users and carers
- Includes the need to involve the patient and their carers from the outset in planning for the patient's discharge, including the provision of any training the carer may need to take over the patient's care
- Is agreed and circulated widely within and beyond the hospital
                    Source: National Audit Office 2000, p. 85

Also in 2000, a team of researchers from the University of York published findings of a systematic literature review looking at the appropriateness with which acute beds are used (McDonagh *et al.* 2000). Although a range of methodological difficulties exist (*see* Appendix A), the authors concluded that a substantial number of bed days may be lost each year due to delayed hospital discharges (*see* Table 5.3).

Table 5.3: Inappropriate bed use*

User group	Rate of inappropriate bed use (%)	Key factors
Psychiatric patients	24–58	Lack of alternative services (especially housing)
Older people	6–78 (but probably approximately 20)	Lack of alternative services (especially long-term care)
General adult population	5.5–62	–
Paediatrics	12–40	–
Neurological diagnoses	15–36	Awaiting housing adaptations or nursing home place; lack of physiotherapy outpatient services
HIV/AIDS	32	Medical needs that could not be met at home

*Adapted from McDonagh *et al.* 2000.

In the same year, a study of delayed discharges in three hospitals found that just over one-quarter of the sample (456 patients admitted from home and discharged from designated elderly care wards between February and September 1997) had a recorded delay in their case notes of three days or more (Victor *et al.* 2000). Although approximately 40% were delayed beyond the date that the clinician deemed them 'medically fit for discharge', the definition of 'delay' varied between hospitals and ward staff often felt that the definition of 'medically fit for discharge' was quite stringent, not necessarily reflecting the date when a patient could actually be discharged. Above all, the researchers found that one individual and two organisational factors were particularly associated with delayed discharge.

- *The organisation of the hospital elderly care team*: late referrals to social care and the lack of emphasis on multi-disciplinary assessment may delay discharge.
- *Entry into residential or nursing care*: this is an important decision for older patients and may take time. Comprehensive assessment also involves a range of different health and social care professionals, and residential/nursing home staff may visit the older person in hospital. Making a placement in institutional forms of care may also require senior management approval within the SSD, and it may take time for a vacancy in a suitable home to become available.
- *The absence of a family carer*: without a family carer, patients cannot be discharged home until they are able to manage independently or

with support from community services. Carers may also be key figures in the decision-making process when an older person enters residential or nursing care, and the absence of such a person may delay finding an appropriate placement.

Also in 2000, a further contribution to the hospital discharge debate was made by Health and Older People (HOPe) in a report on older people's experiences of health and social care (HOPe 2000). Supported by Help the Aged, HOPe is an independent group of 15 people, all but one of whom are over the age of retirement. Although not claiming to be representative of any specific organisation, members of HOPe are drawn from a wide range of local and national voluntary groups and feel that the document in question reflects the experiences of older people more generally throughout England. Although the standards set out by HOPe cover topics ranging from home care to transport and from rehabilitation to preparing for death, the report does comment specifically on older people's expectations with regard to hospital discharge (HOPe 2000, p. 12):

> Discharge from hospital should never take place without proper preparation for the patient and without services at home being in place. The patient and their family should be involved in deciding on the appropriate arrangements, and this is one of the times when an independent advocate may be particularly important. Family members should not be required to take on unfamiliar nursing tasks without support and help on hand. Nursing and personal care need to be in place for older people who live alone when they return from hospital. Older people should never be sent straight from hospital to permanent places in residential or nursing homes without proper consideration having been given to rehabilitation.

In 2001, the House of Commons Select Committee on Public Accounts produced a report, *Inpatient Admission, Bed Management and Patient Discharge in NHS Acute Hospitals*. Reiterating the findings of the National Audit Office (2000), the Select Committee concluded that:

> ... over 2 million bed days are lost each year because of delays in discharging people from hospital. On any given day, some 6000 people aged 75 and over who were ready for discharge were delayed, thereby blocking beds and costing hospitals around £1 million a day. (House of Commons Select Committee on Public Accounts 2001, para. 3 and 42)

Key internal factors contributing to this situation included the timing of consultants' decisions and delays in providing 'take-home' drugs or transport. However, many delayed discharges were also caused by delays in assessing the needs of older patients and in securing appropriate care packages in the community or in residential or nursing care. As a result, partnership between health and social care was seen as crucial to securing timely and effective hospital discharge (House of Commons Select Committee on Public Accounts 2001, para. 44–45 and 51):

> The [NHS] Executive assured us that the partnership between the Health Service and Social Services had improved enormously. There was a seam between the services, and there was a need for an integrated health and social services system that worked for patients … While the Executive were trying to integrate the services, the system did nevertheless operate with two cheque books, and local government had other legitimate priorities that might affect social care budgets. There were variations around the country in where the lines were drawn between health and social care. The Executive could lay down some ground rules, for example that avoided conflict between health authorities and local authorities over who was going to fund a daily visit to someone to help them bathe properly and get dressed. But a more fundamental redrawing of the boundary between health and social care was complex and political … Providing good quality services to patients depends crucially on a strong partnership between hospitals, general practitioners and social services departments.

Also in 2001, a SSI report on social care services for older people found ongoing evidence of difficulties concerning hospital discharge. Based on a national inspection of 21 local authorities, input from staff and a survey of users and carers, the study found that some older people had to stay in hospital longer than was necessary due to shortages in social services funding (Department of Health/SSI 2001, p. 14):

> Sometimes older people [awaiting a residential or nursing home placement] waited for funding in a hospital bed. This could be a particularly poor experience for the older person, who typically would worry how long they would have to wait and had a poorer quality of life living on a ward than they would have had living in the home.

In addition to funding problems, some delayed discharges were the result of older patients waiting for a vacancy in the care home of their choice or of insufficient capacity and specialist skills within local care homes. In some cases, such delays created tensions between health and social services staff and some workers found hospital discharge to be one of the most problematic areas of partnership working (Department of Health/SSI 2001, p. 29):

> Joint work between social services and NHS colleagues around discharge was sometimes the area of partnership work that was seen by the social services staff involved to be working least well because of the dynamic resulting from delayed discharges. In our survey of social services staff …, 68 per cent said that general arrangements for working with the NHS were good or very good but only 49 per cent said that arrangements for hospital admission and discharge were good or very good.

In the same year, Carers UK published the results of two studies conducted as part of its Carers' Health Matters campaign (Hill and Macgregor 2001; Holzhausen 2001). Updating the research of Henwood (1998), *You Can Take Him Home Now* (Holzhausen 2001) explored carers' experiences of hospital discharge via a questionnaire completed by some 2215 people.

Of these carers, 28% reported a good experience of hospital discharge, with the remaining 72% reporting poor experiences. Significantly, one of the key findings from this study was that carers' experience of hospital discharge, far from improving, was worse in a number of important areas than it had been in Henwood's (1998) research (*see* Table 5.4). Key issues included a lack of choice about taking on caring responsibilities, lack of consultation with carers about discharge plans, readmissions to hospital owing to premature discharge, a failure to assess the needs of some carers and a lack of support at home after discharge. In addition, the study found that carers from ethnic minorities fared less well than white carers, women fared less well than men and younger carers fared less well than older carers (Holzhausen 2001, pp. 3–4):

> Overall, compared to white carers, [carers from ethnic minorities] were less likely to be consulted (56% to 64%), more likely not to have their concerns taken into account (52% to 45%) or to be involved in the planning process (23% to 34%) … Higher proportions of carers from ethnic minorities (49% compared to 38%) felt that the person they cared for was not sent home at the right time and higher proportions, six out of ten carers, were not given sufficient support in the home following hospital discharge …

> The results indicate that the older the carer, the more likely they were to feel that their concerns and comments had been taken on board. Those most likely to report they had been consulted were carers aged between 76 and 85 (74%) and those least likely were carers aged 26 to 35 (50%). The younger the carer, the more likely there was to be a readmission to hospital within two months. Far higher proportions of older carers thought that the person they cared for had been sent home at the right time (81% aged over 85 compared to 59% of carers aged between 26 and 35). Higher proportions of older carers had received carer's assessments. Fewer younger carers said they were given sufficient support on returning home …

> While many responses to questions were similar, several differences between the genders were apparent. Forty per cent of male carers were involved in planning the discharge compared to 31% of women. Fifty five per cent of men had their needs assessed compared to 47% of women and 64% of men said that they had sufficient support when the person they cared for returned home compared to 54% of women.

When asked to recommend a single piece of action to improve carers' experiences of hospital discharge, the carers identified the following issues:

- listen to the carer
- ensure the carer has information on the illness, available support services and is signposted to sources of benefits information, etc.
- ensure that there are sufficient support services in place on discharge
- give sufficient notice of, and be flexible about, timing of the discharge
- ensure the patient is not discharged too soon
- improve co-ordination between health and social care, and between departments within the NHS

- ensure that vital equipment is available at the point of discharge
- do not assume that carers can cope, allow them a choice
- ensure that there is one point of contact
- improve the transport arrangements from hospital.

Table 5.4: Carers' experiences of hospital discharge*

Experience of discharge	Percentage of carers (1998)	Percentage of carers (2001)
Carers felt they had no choice about taking on the caring responsibility when the person they were caring for left hospital	71	70
Carers said they were consulted about hospital discharge plans	71	64
People being cared for readmitted to hospital within two months of discharge	25	27
Received an assessment of their needs as carers	40	50
Carers not given sufficient support when the person they cared for returned home from hospital	–	43

*Adapted from Holzhausen (2001).

As a follow up to this research, *Health's Forgotten Partners* (Hill and Macgregor 2001) reviewed the discharge policies of 23 acute hospital trusts in the north-west of England in order to identify the extent to which they address the needs of carers. Once again, a range of similar issues was to emerge from this analysis, including a lack of emphasis on consulting carers about discharge and a more general failure to recognise their needs during the discharge process (*see* Table 5.5). Very few discharge policies had been developed in conjunction with carers' organisations and 70% of trusts gave no explanation as to how they would be monitored and updated. Overall, the researchers concluded that (Hill and Macgregor 2001, p. 7):

> There is a clear gap between Government policy and carers' experiences of hospital discharge. Evidence suggests that NHS Trusts are not putting policy into practice that identifies and supports carers. Whilst discharge policies recognise that carers need to be fully involved in the hospital discharge process, few seem to have put in place practical measures to support them ... Hospital Trusts and Social Services, in conjunction with carers, need to review their discharge policies in light of this research and the findings of *You Can Take Him Home Now*. Reshaped policies will require staff training to ensure proper implementation, backed up by effective monitoring to ensure that practice is consistent throughout the Trust and focusing on whether outcomes for carers have been met. The Government has signalled that their policy on hospital discharge will be updated shortly. This research and *You Can Take Him Home Now* illustrate that new policy must address support for carers. There is concern, however, that guidance and workbooks have

not yet delivered real improvements for carers ... [As a result] the Government needs to consider whether legislation is required to deliver significant changes and provide carers with legal recourse.

Table 5.5: Hospital discharge policies and carers*

Needs of carers	Percentage of hospital discharge policies referring to carers' needs
Users and carers should be central to the discharge process	91
Carers should be involved in discharge planning prior to admission	48
Carers should receive training or instruction on the use of equipment and how to care for it	39
Carers should receive a written copy of discharge plans	35
Carers should be informed of the complaints process	26
There is a need to identify relatives or friends who do not define themselves as 'carers'	22
Carers or carers' organisations should be involved in establishing hospital discharge policies	17
Carers have a right to an assessment of their needs as carers	13
Carers should have a choice about caring	4
Follow-up arrangements should be made to ensure that care arranged in hospital is meeting carers' needs	<1

*Adapted from Hill and Macgregor (2001).

Late in 2001, the Social Policy Ageing Information Network (SPAIN) published its analysis of social care funding and the consequences of financial shortages for older people (SPAIN 2001). Made up of representatives from a range of agencies concerned with services for older people, SPAIN was extremely critical of what it saw as the long-term underfunding of social care. Citing a number of practical examples of what can happen when funding problems prevent older people from leaving hospital (*see* Box 5.6), the report sought to highlight the effect that this could have on other areas of the health and social care system (SPAIN 2001, p. 7):

> Underfunding of social care leads to back-ups and bottlenecks in the health care system which jeopardises [government policies]. People are stuck in hospital awaiting social care funding – an inappropriate place for them to be. Consequently, there is increased pressure on hospital beds and longer waiting times for other patients. Older people in hospital are pressured into taking up inappropriate residential or nursing home beds in order to free a bed, and thereby denied choice in what could be a decision affecting the rest of their lives.

Box 5.6   Delayed discharge case studies

Mrs K has been in hospital for 25 weeks, awaiting discharge to her home. She has been assessed as needing two care workers four times a day but due to understaffing she has been placed on a waiting list … She is extremely depressed in hospital. August 2001

Mrs B's mother-in-law was assessed as needing residential care while in hospital in November 2000. The financial assessment has yet to be carried out. She has remained in hospital the whole time … Funding can only be arranged when a currently funded resident 'no longer requires help' or extra resources are allocated by the government. July 2001

Mr M's mother is 93 and has been in hospital since February. She has been assessed as needing residential care, has no property to sell and has savings of below £11,500. Mr M has been told by the Social Services Department that there is a 6 month wait for residential care funding … July 2001

Mrs Z is in hospital and has been assessed as needing a further night call once she returns home. The Social Services Department has said that there are insufficient resources to provide this extra call and advised her of her right to use the formal complaints procedure. September 2001

Mr T's mother has been in hospital for six months awaiting Social Services funding for a care home. The Social Services Department [says] that funds are not available for this at present. He has made a formal complaint, contacted the MP and press and sent letters from a solicitor but to no avail. June 2001

Mrs R has dementia and needs a hoist. Her husband was told by Social Services that it would have taken a minimum of 9 months to get a hoist. This would have resulted in his wife remaining in hospital for that length of time. Mr R approached us for help with purchasing the hoist. June 2001

Mr C was in hospital and assessed as needing a nursing home. The consultant said that only a few homes were capable of providing the level of care needed. The family were told that the social services limit [was] £346, which was substantially lower than the cost of suitable homes …

Mrs P is in hospital awaiting an assessment. The Social Services Department has advised her daughter that if her mother returns home, it can no longer afford to provide her with her previous domiciliary care package or any additional care she now needs. They have also said

continued overleaf

that they 'will not be able to afford to pay any residential care fees' ...
July 2001

Mr A is in hospital following a stroke. The Social Services Department has assessed him as needing grab rails to help him with bathing when he returns home, but has said that they no longer provide such items. June 2001

Mrs H had been in hospital for over 6 months and had been assessed as needing a nursing home. The family identified a suitable, local home but the council said that it was above their funding level.

Source: SPAIN 2001, pp. 17–18

Also in late 2001, Care and Repair England published a guide on the role of home improvement agencies (HIAs) in facilitating hospital discharge (Adams 2001, pp. 4 and 12):

> Most people wish to stay in their own homes for as long as possible but need assistance to address the problems of old or unsuitable housing. Home improvement agencies ... provide the help necessary to enable older, disabled and other low income homeowners to tackle their housing repair and adaptation problems, thereby enabling them to remain in their own homes. Clearly HIAs have a great deal to offer anyone living in an unfit home or one which is no longer suitable for their needs due to a physical disability, whether or not they are being discharged from hospital ... The hospital discharge services provided by HIAs usually aim to help people who are unable to leave hospital and return to their own homes until an essential adaptation or repair is carried out. Most agencies help mainly older people living in owner occupied or private rented accommodation, though most do some work across tenure and age groups. The actual help provided to achieve this broad aim and the extent of the service varies significantly. Some small scale schemes are literally fast track adaptations services whereby hospital occupational therapists (OTs) put through requests for the installation of a specified item (such as a handrail) which is then organised very quickly either via a group of contractors or an in-house handyperson or technician service. In other cases the hospital discharge service is more comprehensive and undertakes all of the functions of the core HIA service but uses fast track methods to meet the person's most pressing ... needs. The person can then return home and continue to live in the house whilst more major work is undertaken.

Having reviewed the housing, health and social care policy context and described different types of hospital discharge service run by agencies such as Age Concern and the Red Cross, the report describes a series of practical housing projects working in this area (*see* Box 5.7). Next, the guide offers a series of recommendations for those seeking to develop a hospital discharge HIA project, focusing on matters such as planning, funding, practical considerations, sustainability, service agreements and the use of data for monitoring purposes. Advice is also presented from existing projects as to what makes a good HIA hospital discharge scheme (Adams 2001, pp. 28–30):

- rapid access to money to pay for work to the person's home is critical
- you need to be able to do small jobs very fast
- it is important to spend time developing positive working relationships with hospital staff and to establish a shared commitment to making the service work for patients
- a good hospital discharge scheme needs to demonstrate a flexible approach and be willing to innovate and to change systems.

Box 5.7   Hospital discharge home improvement agency projects

Upon leaving hospital, most people return to a decent, comfortable home and are cared for by relatives and friends. But for many older and disabled people this is not the case and going home from hospital can be a difficult time. Help may be needed with basic day to day tasks which most of us take for granted; getting washed and dressed, cooking, cleaning and shopping suddenly all become major hurdles. Trying to manage all of this in a home which is cold, damp, draughty and unsafe is even harder. For people who are leaving hospital with reduced mobility or a new physical impairment, adaptations to their homes can make or break efforts to live with dignity and regain an independent life. This is why the work of home improvement agencies to help people who are leaving hospital is so valuable.

Source: Professor Ian Philp, National Director for Older People, Department of Health, quoted in Adams 2001

At Hackney Staying Put Discharge Scheme staff carry out a range of adaptations and repairs in order to enable older people to return home from hospital. The project has a dedicated fund for meeting the cost of small repairs/adaptations and also provides benefit checks.

The Warwick Daily Living Support Scheme provides short-term domiciliary services, offers advice on equipment and carries out small adaptations.

Coventry Care and Repair Hospital Link Discharge Scheme provides a fast track adaptations service and a home safety assessment to reduce the likelihood of hospital re-admissions.

Bristol Care and Repair Hospital Discharge and Admission Prevention Service provides a repairs, adaptations and support service. An independent evaluation has highlighted the role of the project in preventing delayed hospital discharges.

Source: Adams 2001, preface and pp. 13–20

Significantly the Care and Repair England study was launched on 13 February 2002, the same day on which the House of Commons Health Committee began an investigation of delayed hospital discharges. When the Committee reported its findings in July 2002, its report, *Delayed Discharges*, represented one of the most up-to-date and comprehensive documents available on this problematic area of policy and practice. Having analysed the extent and causes of delayed discharges, the Committee concluded that in the second quarter of 2001–2002 there were 7065 delayed discharges of people of all ages. This represents 6% of all acute beds and may cost the NHS approximately £720 million per annum. In seeking to resolve this situation, the Committee made a series of recommendations, including the need for:

- action to prevent unnecessary hospital admissions
- a named person to co-ordinate all stages of the patient journey through hospital, up to and beyond discharge; this could take the form of a multidisciplinary discharge liaison team, with a leader jointly appointed by the NHS and the SSD
- a range of practical measures to reduce delays caused by internal hospital issues; key issues include the need for earlier planning, the timing of consultant ward rounds, take-home medication, transport, discharge lounges and discharge co-ordinators
- new government guidance on hospital discharge
- a reconfiguration of services to avoid inappropriate admissions and facilitate timely discharges
- interim care arrangements to be made for patients waiting to enter the care home of their choice
- a greater emphasis on supported housing and on the provision of aids and adaptations
- the development of new technology (such as telemonitoring and telemedicine)
- whole systems approaches to hospital discharge.

Above all, however, the Committee repeated its previous (1999) emphasis on the need for integrated health and social care services as the only long-term solution to the difficulties associated with delayed hospital discharges (House of Commons Health Committee 2002, p. 58):

> The evidence we have heard simply strengthens our view, stated in our predecessor Committee's inquiry into the relationship between health and social services ..., that the problems of collaboration between health and social services will not be properly resolved until there is an integrated health and social care system, whether this is in the NHS, within local government or within some new separate organisation. We recognise that [recent government initiatives] all add to the incentives for health and local authorities to work together, but they fall short

of unifying the two agencies ... For many years there has been insistent exhortation for these bodies to work together. Unless there is a rapid change and clear evidence that the challenges of delayed discharges are being effectively managed by joint working, it will be further proof that leads to the inescapable conclusion that radical structural reform is required.

In addition, a statistical overview of delayed discharges is available via data collected by the Department of Health as part of the current performance assessment regime. At the time of writing, both health and social care supply data with regard to a series of official performance indicators, thereby enabling comparisons between agencies and over time in specific areas of practice (*see*, for example, Department of Health/Office for National Statistics 2001; NHS Executive 2000). Delayed discharge (the percentage of people aged 75 and over in an acute hospital bed whose hospital discharge is delayed) is monitored in both health and social care assessment frameworks, representing what is described as an 'interface indicator' that sheds light on the state of inter-agency working. This is justified by the Department of Health in the following terms (Department of Health/Office for National Statistics 2001, p. 112):

> Hospital discharge marks the boundary between the responsibility of the acute, continuing and community health services of the NHS and councils. Delayed discharge can be a result of poor communication between the relevant care organisations or due to the need to meet an individual's choice. The way in which staff and organisations communicate and co-ordinate is an important component of the quality of services for users and carers.

Although performance has improved slightly since this data was first collected in 1998–1999, the data must be interpreted with caution due to methodological changes in the monitoring process. Overall, however, the Department of Health concludes that 'good performance is low' and that the rate of delayed discharges remains more than 10% (Department of Health/Office for National Statistics 2001, p. 112; *see also* Table 5.6). Between 1998 and 2001, this has meant that anywhere from 5000 to almost 7000 people aged 75 and over may be experiencing delayed discharges at any one time (personal communication, NHS Executive 2000). Reasons for delayed discharges include:

- awaiting assessment (21%)
- awaiting SSD funding to residential or nursing home package (14%)
- awaiting non-acute NHS care (for example rehabilitation or continuing care) (10%)
- awaiting nursing or residential home placement (29%)
- awaiting domiciliary care package (8%)
- other reasons (18%).

Table 5.6: Delayed discharges*

Year	Delayed discharges (percentage of people aged 75 and over in an acute hospital bed whose hospital discharge is delayed)
1998–1999	13.1
1999–2000	11.4
2000–2001	11.3

*Adapted from Department of Health/Office for National Statistics 2001, p. 112.

Building on these and other figures, a further contribution has also been made by the Liberal Democrats, whose shadow minister for older people has highlighted the prevalence of delayed hospital discharges, the human cost of such a situation and the impact on the effective functioning of the NHS (*see*, for example, Burstow, n.d.; Liberal Democrats 2002a, 2002b, 2002c). Although this material may not always be dispassionately presented, it does summarise many of the key issues in a striking and explicit fashion. Entitled *No Room at the Inn*, Burstow's report identifies a 'care gridlock' which leaves many older patients in 'limbo' as they wait to be discharged from hospital (Burstow, n.d.). According to Burstow's analysis, 21 522 people aged 75 and over experienced a delayed hospital discharge between April 1999 and March 2000, with an overall increase of 13% between April 1999 and March 2001. In human terms, this leads to an increased risk of hospital-acquired infections, a decline in staff morale, rising readmissions to hospital and a knock-on effect on other hospital departments, with patients in Accident and Emergency sometimes unable to transfer to surgical or medical wards. For the NHS, Burstow calculates that delayed discharges may lose the NHS 1400 years of hospital bed time, that 88 000 operations will have been lost to the NHS between April 2001 and June 2002, and that delayed discharges cost the NHS £23 500 000 a quarter (Liberal Democrats 2002a, 2002b, 2002c). Turning these figures to full political advantage, Burstow then goes on to call the government to account for its handling of health and social care in a manner with which many practitioners and managers may well be able to identify:

> Every year there are [a substantial number of] elderly people well enough to leave but stuck in hospital because the care is not available. This means, at its most grotesque, waiting in hospital for someone to die in a care home, before the Council will fund a new placement! These people are labelled as bed blockers as if it is their fault! It is the Government's fault. (Liberal Democrats 2002a, p. 1)

> Every year, thousands of elderly people are well enough to leave hospital, but have to remain because social services do not have the resources to care for them after they have been discharged. At its worst, the system leaves people waiting in hospitals until someone else dies in a care home, before the Council will fund

a new care place. Ministers are stuck in a state of denial about the crisis in the care system. They have failed to grasp the scale of staff shortages, care home closures and the loss of home care services. (Liberal Democrats 2000b, p. 1)

The victims of bed blocking are the frail elderly who find themselves caught-up in a game of pass the parcel between health and social care ... Taxpayers' money is wasted on keeping people in NHS beds when what they want is good care at home or a place in a care home. (Liberal Democrats 2002c, p. 1)

Other examples

Whereas this book has focused primarily on services in England and on the experiences of older people, there is also a considerable body of literature on hospital discharge in other areas of the UK and on the discharge of other user groups. Although this literature is not reviewed in as much detail as the research studies outlined above, a brief overview of the available research reveals that the experience of older people in England is remarkably similar to that of other user groups and of people in Northern Ireland, Scotland and Wales.

In Northern Ireland, health and social services have traditionally been more integrated than in the rest of the UK (*see*, for example, Department of Health, Social Services and Public Safety (DHSSPS/SSI 2000). Instead of local authority SSDs administered separately from a centrally organised healthcare system (the approach adopted in England), Northern Ireland has four health and social services boards, overseen by the Department of Health, Social Services and Public Safety (DHSSPS), which commission both health and social care from a range of acute and community trusts. Despite this, the evidence from a multi-disciplinary inspection of hospital discharge arrangements in four health and social services trusts reveals a number of ongoing problems (DHSSPS/SSI 1997). With fieldwork conducted in early 1997, the SSI recognised that its inspection was taking place at a time when health and social services were experiencing a range of challenges in responding to the needs of older people with complex needs (DHSSPS/SSI 1997, p. 5):

- the need to have effective discharge arrangements that managed the tension between ensuring that patients receive a comprehensive assessment of need and avoiding the effect on hospital resources of undue discharge delays
- implementing clear and effective care management arrangements and providing timely and appropriate interventions that have been agreed with users and carers
- managing the change and increase in the workload created for professionals since the introduction of assessment and care management

- managing the interface between hospital and community and developing a collaborative approach to multi-disciplinary working
- working with a climate of increasing financial constraints and providing sufficient and appropriate resources to meet users' needs, enabling discharge to take place.

Although hospital discharge arrangements existed in each of the four hospital sites inspected, it was found that there was wide variation in practice in terms of assessment, care planning, discharge and review. In two areas, trusts had not developed their protocols in conjunction with all professional disciplines and the resulting procedures lacked shared ownership. This was not aided by the absence of ongoing multi-disciplinary training, by the failure to disseminate information to some front-line members of staff or patients and by the variability of mechanisms developed to monitor hospital discharge arrangements. At the same time, variations in eligibility criteria within and across health and social services boards caused confusion for staff, whereas the lack of formal information-sharing mechanisms could result in medical and nursing staff not receiving sufficient feedback on referrals. Further concerns included lack of clarity about budget allocations in a number of trusts, lack of involvement of community nurses or OTs in discharge planning, failure to conduct separate carers' assessments and lack of rehabilitation or convalescence services (*see* Box 5.8 for a summary of key findings). Overall, the inspectors concluded that (DHSSPS/SSI 1997, p. 5):

> It is essential that professionals understand each other's skills and work effectively together in order to provide appropriate and timely intervention to both patients and carers. The establishment and implementation of a collaborative approach to hospital discharge arrangements will contribute to a seamless service and a smooth transfer from hospital to community or residential/nursing home care. The findings of this inspection have highlighted wide variations in practice, not only across Boards, but within particular hospital sites. There are a number of major issues that will require to be addressed by Hospital and Community Trusts in order to improve the quality of life and services to older people and their carers on discharge from hospital and to allow best use of Trusts' resources.

Box 5.8   Sample findings from Northern Ireland

- There were wide variations in practice across Boards and within trusts in relation to assessment, care management and discharge arrangements ...
- Eligibility criteria for screening, assessment and care management varied both within and across Board areas, which resulted in confusion for staff and raised issues regarding equity of service provision within some hospital sites.

continued opposite

- Published information on assessment, care management and discharge arrangements was inadequate in a number of Trusts …
- The assessment, care planning and review process did not always reflect the full consultation and participation of users, carers and professionals …
- It was the view of some hospital professionals that medical staff, on general hospital wards, were not sufficiently involved in, or informed about assessment, care management and discharge procedures …
- The procedures for identifying and collating unmet need were not known by the full range of professional staff …
- Examples of good practice were identified, most notably where services were activated in advance of discharge and opportunities were provided for older people to test out equipment in their own home with professional support.
- There was evidence of effective multi-disciplinary working arrangements on rehabilitation wards and wards for the care of the elderly …
- Many users interviewed expressed satisfaction with the services they received, although some carers were dissatisfied with the Trusts' restricted funding for care packages and inadequate time available to make informed decisions regarding residential placements …
- A number of patients in several Trusts, who have been assessed and care managed, cannot be discharged from hospital as funding is not available to deliver their agreed care package …
- Training was provided in the early stages of the community care reforms although ongoing multi-disciplinary training was not in place for all staff involved in assessment, care management and discharge arrangements.

Source: DHSSPS/SSI 1997, pp. 5–8

In Scotland, research conducted by the Scottish Executive Central Research Unit has already been cited above and suggests that hospital discharge can sometimes be problematic for older people in Scotland as well as in England (Taraborrelli *et al.* 1998). A key contribution has also been made by researchers from the Nursing Research Unit at the University of Edinburgh (*see*, for example, Tierney *et al.* 1993b and Chapter 4). In addition to this, however, a series of national censuses of patients ready for discharge has been conducted since 30 September 2000 by the Information and Statistics Division (ISD) following a management executive letter issued by the Scottish Executive Health Department (ISD Scotland 2000, 2001a, 2001b, 2001c, 2002). Over time, this data provides an overview of the number of patients waiting to leave hospital and the main reasons for delay (*see* Tables 5.7 and 5.8). The top five causes of delayed discharge have consistently been found to include:

• awaiting commencement or completion of post-hospital social care assessment
• non-availability of public funding for nursing home place
• awaiting place availability in nursing home (not NHS-funded)
• awaiting bed availability in other NHS hospital/specialty/facility
• patient exercising statutory right of choice (that is, over which residential or nursing home to enter).

As part of action to tackle the issue of delayed discharges, the Scottish Minister for Health established a working group in July 2000 to look into developing a learning network for delayed discharges (Scottish Executive 2000). Building on the work of a short-life Winter Performance Group launched in September 2000, the group identified a series of key issues to consider and made a number of recommendations (*see* Box 5.9). In addition, the group also highlighted key local differences across Scotland (such as geography, population profile, service configuration and so on) and identified a series of examples of good practice. Further support for action to tackle delayed discharges has also come from the Scottish Executive's Care Development Group, which called for multi-disciplinary programmes to prevent unnecessary hospital admissions, facilitate discharge and increase the level of recuperation and rehabilitation services available. Crucially, the Group saw delayed hospital discharge both as an individual problem for patients unable to return home and as an organisational problem for the NHS (Care Development Group 2001, p. 20):

> One of the major and most immediate issues facing care services is the number of hospital beds which are being occupied by older people who no longer need NHS care. There were in April, ... 1900 people who had been waiting more than 6 weeks to leave hospital. Some have been waiting for months. Keeping older people in hospital long after they are ready to go out is counter-productive. It denies the individual the care appropriate to their needs. Moreover, because they are not in an appropriate environment it runs the very real risk of them deteriorating to the point where they cannot contemplate going home or indeed going on to some form of residential care. The whole experience of acute intervention and hospitalisation can be very destabilising to anxious older people, especially those bewildered by dementia ... This is also a critical issue for the NHS as well as for the individuals concerned. We would never want to reduce our older people to mere statistics or to portray them as a nuisance factor which the NHS has to deal with. Each one of those 1900 people is an individual with family and friends and a life of their own to lead. We cannot however underplay the problems which will face the NHS if suitable arrangements are not made soon to allow those people who are ready to be discharged to move on to a care home, or back to their own home with appropriate support.

Table 5.7:   Patients ready for discharge in Scotland, 2000–2001*

Date of census	Number of patients ready for discharge	Number of patients delayed by more than six weeks
30 September 2000	3021	1944
15 January 2001	2844	1920
15 April 2001	2885	1938
15 July 2001	2954	2019
15 October 2001	3318	2191

*Adapted from ISD Scotland 2000, 2001a, 2001b, 2001c, 2002.

Table 5.8:   Principal causes of delayed discharges*

Main causes of delayed discharge	September 2000 No of patients (%)	January 2001 No of patients (%)	April 2001 No of patients (%)	July 2001 No of patients (%)	October 2001 No of patients (%)
Awaiting start/ completion of post-hospital social care assessment	533 (18.0)	625 (22.1)	586 (20.3)	613 (20.8)	681 (21.7)
Non-availability of public funding for nursing home place	645 (21.8)	423 (15.0)	491 (17.0)	506 (17.1)	546 (17.4)
Awaiting place availability in nursing home (not NHS-funded)	244 (8.2)	322 (11.4)	326 (11.3)	388 (13.1)	398 (12.7)
Awaiting bed availability in other NHS hospital/specialty/ facility	252 (8.5)	261 (9.2)	188 (6.5)	213 (7.2)	249 (7.9)
Patient exercising statutory right of choice	153 (5.2)	138 (4.9)	160 (5.5)	171 (5.8)	158 (5.0)

*Adapted from ISD Scotland 2000, 2001a, 2001b, 2001c, 2002.

Box 5.9 Tackling delayed discharges in Scotland

There is no single solution to the problem of delayed discharges. However, there are a number of key issues which it is essential to consider when developing plans to address delayed discharges. The key issues include:

- An effective framework for managing older people's health and social care needs.
- An approach to managing health problems including preventing admission with effective crisis support in the community and effective discharge arrangements so that acute admissions of older people are not delayed in hospital.
- Effective discharge arrangements within hospitals and between health and social work.
- Effective management of complex packages of care for older people in the community.
- Integrated health and social care both for strategic planning, operational planning and the provision of services.
- Good relationships between key statutory agencies at an individual and corporate level.
- Effective clear communications between professionals and with the users of services.
- Adequate and varied supply of alternative service provision outside of hospital in particular nursing home provision.

... Recommendations to establish a learning network ... are summarised below:

- A network should be established to enable exchange of good practice and effective ways of working on delayed discharges. While recognising the impact of local circumstances, lessons from different areas are transferable.
- The network should involve both a web site of information and also workshops and conferences to allow discussion and training.
- The ISD data collection should be developed to enable effective comparisons and performance management across Health Board areas.
- A National Service Framework for Services to Older People should be developed for Scotland that would incorporate the issues pertinent to delayed discharges.

Source: Scottish Executive 2000, pp. 1–2 and 13

In Wales, delayed transfers of care have been monitored monthly since December 2000, with all NHS hospitals identifying every patient experiencing a delayed transfer of care (including discharge) and the principal reason for this. A delayed transfer of care is experienced when 'an inpatient occupying a specialty/significant facility bed in a hospital, who is ready to move on to the next stage of care, ... is prevented from doing so by one or more reasons' (National Assembly for Wales 2000, p. 1). The reasons for delayed transfers of care are agreed with the local SSD and recorded on the basis of approximately 40 numerical codes which focus on:

- *Healthcare reasons* (such as a change in the patient's health circumstances, awaiting completion of a post-hospital health assessment by various professionals, awaiting bed availability in other NHS hospital, etc.).
- *Social care reasons* (awaiting completion of community care assessment, awaiting funding for residential or nursing care, awaiting rehousing, etc.).
- *Patient/carer/family-related reasons* (legal issues, financial problems, internal family dispute, etc.).

Although the results of this monitoring process are not in the public domain at the time of writing, the principal causes of delayed transfers include (personal communication, National Assembly for Wales):

- awaiting funding agreement from the local authority for residential or nursing home care provision
- awaiting place availability and completion of relevant social care arrangements in residential care home – physical disability/frailty
- awaiting place availability and completion of relevant social care arrangements in nursing home (not NHS-funded)
- awaiting bed availability in other NHS hospital/specialty/facility
- awaiting bed availability in non-NHS hospital/specialty/facility (e.g. hospice, continuing care bed in nursing home)
- other patient/carer/family-related reasons.

For user groups other than older people, the available evidence suggests that hospital discharge can be a problematic process, both in acute hospitals and in specialist services for people with mental health problems or learning difficulties. Already, this chapter has cited research focusing on the often negative experiences of carers, many of whom feel taken for granted and excluded from the discharge planning process (*see*, for example, Henwood 1998; Hill and Macgregor 2001; Holzhausen 2001). The systematic literature review undertaken by workers at the University of York also suggests that delayed discharges may be common among groups such as children, general adults, mental health service users, people with neurological conditions and people with HIV/AIDS (McDonagh *et al.* 2000). Elsewhere, research conducted by Koffman *et al.* (1996) has found that approximately one-quarter of patients occupying 'elderly–mentally ill' acute and assessment beds in mental health units within the North and South Thames Regions no longer required acute care and were inappropriately located in hospital. A key issue was the lack of alternative services, such as nursing or residential care, and support at home. Many of the patients concerned had dementia and required high levels of supervision, prompting the researchers to question whether existing services were geared to meeting the needs of this particular user group.

In addition, hospital discharge has also been found to be problematic for people in acute psychiatric services. Thus, in one study by the Sainsbury Centre for Mental Health, a one-day census of 38 acute psychiatric wards suggested that 25% of the 559 patients involved did not need acute care (Moore 1998). Key barriers to discharge included a lack of suitable accommodation (32% of patients), a lack of rehabilitation places (22%) and a lack of domiciliary support (19%), with 10% of patients requiring a higher level of support than could be offered on the ward. In stage two of this study, more detailed research with 215 patients from nine hospital wards found that 19% of patients were considered by staff not to need acute care after the first week of their stay. By the end of the second week, this figure had risen to 45% of patients (Sainsbury Centre for Mental Health 1998). Key factors contributing to delayed discharge were felt to include a lack of accommodation, home-based support and rehabilitation places. In most cases, discharge arrangements tended to be made after ad hoc discussions during ward rounds, with only 34% of patients receiving any kind of formal or separate meeting to discuss their after-care. Even those meetings that did take place were poorly attended by community staff and by patients' carers, and most participants in the research 'had no idea they were about to be discharged until a few days before they left, and had little involvement in the discussions about their future' (Sainsbury Centre for Mental Health 1998, p. 33). Overall, the study concluded that 'bed management was currently poor, with large numbers of patients remaining in beds when they did not require inpatient care', calling for more effective discharge planning and greater involvement of patients and carers. Similar findings have also emerged from other studies, which suggest that between 10% and 61% of mental health service users may have their discharge delayed and that many people may not have formally agreed discharge plans on leaving hospital (*see* Table 5.9). The same may also be true of people in secure mental health units, with between 37% and 75% of patients not requiring the services provided in these settings (*see* Glasby *et al.* 2003 for further details).

Table 5.9:   Delayed hospital discharges and mental health*

Study	Delayed discharges (% of patients)	Causes/possible alternatives
Fulop *et al.* (1992)	37	Lack of accommodation and long-stay hospital care
Lelliot *et al.* (1994)	61	Lack of continuing care provision, rehabilitation, supported group homes or low-staffed hostels
Fulop *et al.* (1996)	23	Professional support in the patient's home, housing or more appropriate housing, group homes, rehabilitation
Koffman *et al.* (1996)	24	Residential or nursing home care, total dependency psychiatric care, community services (e.g. day/home care), housing
Connolly and Ritchie (1997)	1994 – 54 1995 – 46	Not reported – delayed discharge figures relate to patients whose admission lasted three months or more
Minghella and Ford (1997)	10% of patients (but 26% of bed days)	Problems finding suitable accommodation (including forensic care)
Sainsbury Centre for Mental Health (1998)	19 (after one week)	Lack of accommodation, lack of home-based support, lack of rehabilitation services, patient required higher levels of supervision
Shepherd *et al.* (1997)	27	Lack of supported housing, lack of rehabilitation services, need for secure accommodation and need for specialist services

Source: Glasby *et al.* 2003; *see also* Bartlett *et al.* 1999; McDonagh *et al.* 2000.

For people with learning difficulties, hospital services have been transformed in recent years, moving away from long-stay institutions to smaller, more specialist units that seek to deal with issues such as mental illness and/or challenging behaviour (often known as assessment and treatment centres). Despite this, there is evidence to suggest that such units are becoming 'blocked' by a 'new long stay population' (*see*, for example, Ballinger *et al.* 1991; Cumella *et al.* 1998; Dickinson and Singh 1991; Khan *et al.* 1993). In one Birmingham-based study, only three out of 21 patients remaining in hospital after more than three months were found to require inpatient care, with the remaining 18 having completed treatment or been assessed as able to continue treatment on an outpatient basis (Cumella *et al.* 1998). In addition to their learning difficulty, most of the 21 patients had psychiatric disorders (16 patients) or autism (five patients), and key characteristics contributing to hospital admission included severe behaviour problems, such as violence to others, self-injury and abnormal sexual behaviour. Although it proved difficult to calculate the mean length of stay beyond treatment needs, the authors estimated that these 18 delayed discharges accounted for expenditure of approximately £750 000. According to hospital staff, key reasons for delay included:

• lack of appropriate residential placements (nine patients)
• lack of appropriate residential accommodation and day care (four patients)
• funding responsibility disputed (five patients).

Although there has been relatively little research on the hospital discharge of younger adults with physical impairments, two key studies do provide an insight into the experiences of this user group. In one study of hospital discharge in the north of England, researchers at the University of York interviewed a sample of carers, patients, practitioners and managers in order to evaluate the effectiveness of discharge procedures for the carers of physically impaired adults and identify possible improvements (Arskey *et al.* 1997). Contrary to previous research, the study found evidence of positive experiences among carers, who were given information and involved in the discharge process. However, there were a number of shortcomings in policy and practice, with carers requesting more wide-ranging information than they received and expressing a wish to be more actively involved in hospital discharge than was the case for some participants. Other key issues included: the tendency to consider patients' needs above those of their carers; a lack of monitoring of carers' experiences of discharge; and concerns about reliability, response times, bureaucracy, continuity of care and the skills of formal carers. Often, carers did not receive a formal assessment of their needs under the Carers (Recognition and Services) Act 1995 and felt that staff prioritised the views of the patient over those of the carer, without recognising that patients and carers may have different needs and priorities. Overall, those carers who voiced concerns about hospital discharge concentrated on the following issues (Arskey *et al.* 1997, p. 81):

• a general lack of information and communication
• no or insufficient meetings with professionals
• promises not kept

- not being adequately prepared (both practically and psychologically) for the patient's discharge.

Also in northern England, research conducted by Acton.Shapiro consultants sought to explore the experiences of 48 disabled people discharged from hospital and 10 carers via a combination of group discussions, one-to-one interviews and written 'discharge stories' (Hare and Newbronner 2001). Although many participants had had good experiences of hospital and of hospital discharge, key areas for improvement included:

- the quality of nursing care on some wards
- a lack of understanding of disability among some members of staff
- the quality and comprehensiveness of information given to patients and their carers
- premature discharge due to pressure on beds
- practical issues, such as arranging medication and transport
- communication difficulties between hospital and community services
- lengthy waiting lists for equipment and adaptations
- a lack of availability for some community services
- the quality of care provided by private agencies.

Summary

Having reviewed a number of research studies that focus on hospital discharge, there is an overwhelming sense of the intractable and persistent nature of many of the problems highlighted by the authors concerned. Over a substantial period of time, the evidence consistently points towards a series of key themes:

- failure to give patients and their carers adequate notice of discharge
- failure to involve patients and their carers in decisions about discharge and ongoing care arrangements
- hospital-based delays in arranging transport or medication
- failure of health and social care practitioners to work effectively together
- the incompatibility of two different systems based on different notions of good practice
- lack of attention to the needs of carers
- the problematic nature of hospital discharge for other user groups and throughout the UK
- structural barriers, such as separate funding streams, and the need to overcome a range of organisational and professional boundaries in order to achieve seamless services.

Crucially, these issues can be seen to fall into three separate but related categories, each of which may require a different policy response:

- At an *individual level* there is a need for action to improve the way that individual practitioners respond to the needs of older patients and communicate with service users, carers and fellow professionals.
- At an *organisational level* there is a need for action by local health and social care agencies to work in partnership, increase their own internal efficiency and develop shared solutions to local problems.
- At a *structural level* there is a need for central government action in order to overcome the financial, legal and administrative obstacles to joint working.

As we have already seen in Chapters 2 and 3, government policy to date has tended to focus more on the individual and organisational levels of hospital discharge than on the underlying structural issues. The only exception to this is in Northern Ireland, where health and social care structures are much more integrated, but where problems at an individual and organisational level still seem to exist. This distinction between individual, organisational and structural factors is discussed in greater detail in Chapter 7, together with policy proposals to improve hospital discharge practice.

CHAPTER 6

Possible solutions

Faced with mounting evidence of the problematic nature of hospital discharge and the contested nature of the boundary between health and social care, policy-makers have developed a range of initiatives designed to promote greater inter-agency collaboration and to ensure more effective use of acute hospital beds. Although many of these have been described in brief in Chapters 2 and 3, this section of the book reviews three specific policies that have potentially extremely significant implications for hospital discharge:

- winter pressures funding
- the *Partnership in Action* proposals enacted under the Health Act 1999
- intermediate care.

In each case, the chapter considers the extent to which the policy in question is likely to contribute to a resolution of the difficulties and complexities described elsewhere in this book with regard to hospital discharge. Although a step in the right direction, it soon becomes apparent that each of the policy initiatives seems insufficient to resolve the deep-rooted issues at stake. By way of conclusion, Chapter 7 makes some alternative proposals for policies that may genuinely overcome some of the problems associated with the hospital discharge of frail older people.

Winter pressures

Although health and social care services are experiencing difficulties all year round, they often face particular pressure in the winter months as conditions become icy and as outbreaks of conditions, such as flu or bronchitis, increase. As a result, it is often at this time of year that journalistic accounts of 'bed blocking' appear in the newspapers as delayed discharges and rising admissions combine to stretch some hospitals to the limit. To the credit of New Labour, one of its earliest health and social care policy initiatives after coming to power in May 1997 was to focus attention very much on the winter pressures faced by the NHS and SSDs. Thus, in August 1997, the then Health Secretary, Frank Dobson, wrote to health and social care agencies outlining his support for front-line workers and underlining the need for joint working (Department of Health 1997a):

> This letter makes clear my determination to ensure that you have the full support of Ministers and officials of the Department of Health in your preparations for managing the pressures on health and local authority services as winter approaches. The coming months will call for truly integrated planning and action. That will mean health authorities, hospitals, community and primary health care staff, social services, housing, ambulance services and independent sector care providers joining forces to plan how to tackle the coming pressures. I know that many of you are already working closely together in this way, but we need to ensure a concerted effort … In particular I expect:
>
> > all agencies to have developed a shared understanding of local sources of any increased demand for hospital services and a realistic strategy to manage it;
> >
> > health authorities and trusts to have planned to optimise the use of available bed capacity including considering with partner agencies what other services need to be available to ensure acute hospital beds are used wisely;
> >
> > to be confident that hospital discharge arrangements deliver an effective and timely outcome for patients – particularly those who need community care support.
>
> I know that you will be tackling all these issues already. In writing now I wish to emphasise my determination to ensure that we are well prepared for the pressures which any winter inevitably brings on health and social services and that we demonstrate our ability to manage these pressures effectively and with care and compassion.

This was followed in October 1997 by a second letter announcing an additional £300 million to ease pressures on the health and social care system during the winter period, restrain the growth in waiting lists/times and deal with a number of forecast overspends (Department of Health 1997b). A similar process also occurred in November 1998, with an additional £250 million of non-recurrent funding pledged to 'ensure that, working closely with Social Services, the NHS manages services effectively over the winter ensuring the capacity to deal with peaks in emergency demand without impeding the progress made in cutting waiting lists' (Department of Health 1998d, p. 2).

Assessing the impact of 'winter pressures' funding is difficult since there has been no national evaluation of the initiative. Despite this, anecdotal evidence from individual winter pressures projects coupled with overall summary documents produced by the Department of Health both begin to suggest that this policy, by itself, might not be enough to overcome the longstanding difficulties associated with the health–social care divide and with the hospital discharge of older people.

In the short term, there seems little doubt that the government's additional funding was very welcome and led to new and often innovative services that facilitated partnership working and helping to improve the quality of care experienced by users and carers. In June 1998, for example, the second report of the Emergency Services Action Team (ESAT) provided an insight into the initial impact of winter pressures funding (ESAT 1998). Set up by the NHS Executive in order to advise on how agencies were preparing for and coping with emergency pressures, ESAT suggested that the new money had been significant in helping health and social care organisations respond to winter pressures (ESAT 1998, para. 8 and 32):

> There is no doubt that early and better planning, the involvement of senior management and the use of winter pressures monies all proved effective in helping the services manage winter pressures better than ever before. As one manager commented to us: 'Last year saw crisis management; this time the crisis was managed and this gave staff at all levels confidence that we could and would cope'... Relationships between Health and Social Services have generally been much better and more productive than in the past. The additional funding helped to increase efficiency of admission and discharge procedures and to initiate new schemes. A good example was the provision of out of hours emergency cover. Arrangements for [the] Christmas/New Year period and other holiday periods was regarded as having worked better than ever before.

Throughout the country, winter pressures monies were used to fund a range of services (*see* Box 6.1). These included schemes to (ESAT 1998, para. 35):

- avoid inappropriate admissions to hospital
- improve hospital management of acute admissions
- reduce intensive care transfers
- improve discharge arrangements to reduce delays
- improve health and social care in the community
- restrain growth in waiting times and lists.

Box 6.1   Winter pressures projects

Whipps Cross Hospital provided an out of hours Senior House Officer in Accident and Emergency.

Queen's Medical Centre in Nottingham attached a pharmacist to the admissions ward so that medicines were available promptly when patients were ready for discharge.

A hospital at home scheme in Redbridge and Waltham Forest maintained 209 patients at home between October 1997 and March 1998, preventing the need for hospital admission.

continued overleaf

Medical assessment units were widely used to assess patients quickly, with between one-quarter and one-third being discharged straight home.

New hospital discharge lounges contributed to major reductions in trolley waits, with fewer patients waiting overnight in Accident and Emergency.

Source: ESAT 1998, para. 38

Often, the new funding was spent on hospital discharge schemes, facilitating flexible partnership working and ensuring that patients were able to receive the community services they required in order to be able to leave hospital safely (*see* Box 6.2).

Box 6.2   Winter pressures and hospital discharge

In Wakefield, £38 000 was invested in the adaptations and disability unit of the local authority in order to facilitate early discharge.

In Bradford, £50 000 has purchased 12 additional nursing home beds to enable earlier discharges. In addition, £30 000 has funded additional medical, nursing and therapy staff to support people discharged from hospital in nursing homes.

In Salisbury, a discharge lounge will free beds by enabling patients ready for discharge to await transport home away from their hospital ward.

Community hospitals in Dorset are to be used for patients who no longer need acute care but who are not yet ready to go home.

Source: Millar 1998

Improved discharge arrangements have also been achieved via:

- discharge co-ordinators
- intermediate care
- intensive rehabilitation
- discharge lounges
- consultants on-call at weekends to discharge patients
- accelerated residential or nursing home places
- additional ambulance staff and vehicles for transfers and discharge at weekend
- hospital at home

continued opposite

- occupational therapists to do pre-discharge home assessments followed by post-discharge physiotherapy
- community trusts working with GPs out of hours
- improved joint collection of delayed discharge information
- purchase of domiciliary care packages
- homefinder schemes
- protocols for post-discharge care by GPs.

Source: ESAT 1998

Despite these many achievements, the new money has not necessarily provided an overall solution to the difficulties associated with hospital discharge. Although very welcome, non-recurrent, short-term funding, such as the winter pressures monies, was probably never going to be sufficient to resolve much more long-term and deep-seated problems, such as the health and social care divide, or the complexity of securing effective multi-agency hospital discharges. With any short-term injection of funds, the danger is always that new initiatives, no matter how successful, may fail to secure ongoing funding and will therefore fail to translate new ways of working into mainstream, accepted practice. This was immediately acknowledged by ESAT and by other bodies, such as the Millennium Executive Team set up to prepare for winter 1999/2000 and the millennium period:

> Irrespective of early indications of effectiveness, only a proportion of all winter pressures schemes were expected to be carried over into 1998/99 as part of core business activity. Of these some were being carried forward using [other external funding sources] to bridge the funding, but concerns were expressed that when budgets are tight investment in community based initiatives was seen as a soft target and vulnerable to cuts irrespective of their input. (ESAT 1998, para. 41)

> In each of the previous two winters, additional funds earmarked for winter pressures had been made available on a non-recurrent basis. While these additional resources were welcomed at a local level, and new services were introduced, the additional resources came late in the planning process and, as funding was non-recurrent, schemes could not always be continued beyond the end of the financial year. (Millennium Executive Team 2000, para. 12)

Elsewhere, other commentators have identified a range of limitations associated with winter pressures funding. For many agencies, insufficient notice led to a situation where detailed planning was extremely difficult, if not impossible. As one social services manager commented (quoted in White 1999, p. 18):

> One of the biggest problems has been the timing of the whole thing. We did not know until November whether we were going to get any extra money at all, let alone how much it would be. This gave us very little time to plan our projects with the local trusts and health authority.

For Age Concern, moreover, winter pressures monies were simply a short-term solution to a much more long-term issue (quoted in White 1999, p. 19):

> It's just a sticking plaster solution to a much deeper problem. The NHS should be able to cope with the extra illness that winter causes. The fact that it can't shows there are more underlying problems. These require long-term funding and long-term strategic thinking.

In addition, it is important to note that some of the winter pressures funding was used to purchase residential or nursing home care for people waiting to be discharged from hospital. Although this may have begun to reduce the backlog of delayed discharges, SSDs who adopted this approach ran the risk of incurring further financial difficulties in the future. Although winter pressures monies may have funded the initial move to residential or nursing homes, such admissions can create ongoing financial liabilities to pay for residents' care for as long as they continue to need a residential or nursing home placement. This can be extremely expensive and can far outweigh the short-term financial gains made by exploiting government money to reduce the number of delayed discharges. As ESAT (1998, para. 78) commented:

> The winter pressures funding did much to improve the admissions and discharge procedures operating between health and social services and provided the spur for innovative new community based schemes. Where there was already large numbers of delayed discharges in the system, however, social services departments came under intense pressure to buy more residential or nursing home beds. We have some real concerns about the continuing reliance on this form of post discharge care:
>
> - using non-recurrent monies to fund long term residential/nursing homes placements simply stores up problems for the future and is likely to undermine efforts to reduce waiting lists. As one manager puts it, 'A nursing home is for life not just for Christmas'.

More recently, the government has responded to these limitations by seeking to provide more sustained funding and by emphasising more long-term year round planning (*see*, for example, Department of Health 2000f, 2001l). However, the fact remains that this early New Labour policy initiative, although very welcome in the short term, was not sufficient to heal the health–social care divide nor to provide a long-term solution to the problematic nature of hospital discharge.

Partnership in Action

Following the introduction of winter pressures funding in 1997, the New Labour government issued a consultation document in September 1998 that sought to explore ways of improving joint working between health and social services (Department of Health 1998a). Entitled *Partnership in Action*, the document provided a scathing critique of the current state of joint working and emphasised the need for urgent change (Department of Health 1998a, p. 3):

> All too often when people have complex needs spanning both health and social care good quality services are sacrificed for sterile arguments about boundaries. When this happens people, often the most vulnerable in our society ... and those who care for them find themselves in the no man's land between health and social services. This is not what people want or need. It places the needs of the organisation above the needs of the people they are there to serve. It is poor organisation, poor practice, poor use of taxpayers' money – it is unacceptable.

Crucially, the government's response to this state of affairs was to rule out widespread reorganisation as a possible way forward, with a very explicit statement on the opening page of the consultation document (Department of Health 1998a, p. 5):

> Major structural change is not the answer. We do not intend to set up new statutory health and social services authorities. They would involve new bureaucracy and would be expensive and disruptive to introduce. Our proposals set out a better course which is less bureaucratic and more efficient for users, for carers, and for staff working in those services who are often as frustrated as the people they are trying to help by the failures of the system.

Instead of major structural reform, the consultation document proposed the creation of three new discretionary 'flexibilities' to remove existing barriers to joint working via:

- *pooled budgets* – funds that lose their health and social care identity and may be spent flexibly by a single pool manager
- *lead commissioning* – where one agency commissions both health and social care for a particular user group
- *integrated provision* – where health and social services are provided together in one-stop shops.

These 'flexibilities' were later enacted under the Health Act 1999 (Department of Health 1999b) and became operational in April 2000. Crucially, the decision as to whether or not to make use of these new powers lay in the hands of local health and social care agencies, who were able to decide if they felt that the new 'flexibilities' were appropriate for the local area. Where the Health Act was implemented locally, agencies had to register their use of the 'flexibilities' with NHS Executive Regional Office. This information was then forwarded to the Joint Health and Social Care Unit of the Department of Health and posted on the Unit's website. More recently, the Health Act 'flexibilities' have received further impetus following the publication of the government's *NHS Plan* (Department of Health 2000a) and the introduction of the Health and Social Care Act 2001 (Department of Health 2001c). Under the latter, PCGs/primary care trusts (PCTs) and local authorities will also be able to apply to the Secretary of State to become Care Trusts – new, hybrid bodies that will be able to commission and provide both health and social care (Department of Health 2001b).

In order to assess the effect of the *Partnership in Action* initiative, the Department of Health commissioned a national evaluation of the Health Act 'flexibilities' from researchers at the Nuffield Institute for Health and the National Primary Care Research and Development Centre (Hudson *et al.* 2001). In the event, use of the new 'flexibilities' was initially much more limited than might have been expected, with only 20 authorities ready to take advantage of the new powers available to them as of 1 April 2000 (Community Care 2000). Hardly surprisingly, this raised key methodological issues for the evaluation, whose interim report stressed the limits of their findings (Hudson *et al.* 2001, pp. 3–4):

> The sites which registered to use the flexibilities in the early months after April 2000 may have had extensive, but relatively unusual, prior histories of joint working, which meant they were ready to use the flexibilities at the earliest possible opportunity. They therefore cannot be assumed to be representative of sites which register their use of the flexibilities at a subsequent date.

Adopting a pluralistic approach, the initial stages of the evaluation were based on a postal questionnaire to the lead contacts of 30 Health Act partnerships (of whom 22 responded), seeking descriptive information about the partnership and requesting key documentation. Next, the researchers sought to assess the strengths and weaknesses of the various partnerships by use of a partnership assessment tool (PAT). Developed by the Nuffield Institute to enable partnership members to assess the overall success of their partnership working, the PAT asks participants to agree or disagree with a number of key statements about how well they are working when compared to six key principles of joint working (*see* Hardy *et al.* 2000 for further details). The response rate to this aspect of the study was approximately 50%, with 49 of 97 partner agencies completing the PAT in the 22 partnerships that responded to the original questionnaire. Future stages of the evaluation will involve more in-depth work via a number of more detailed case studies.

Key findings to emerge from the interim report of the evaluation included (Hudson *et al.* 2001, pp. 11–51):

- Almost half of all notifications came from two regions – Trent and North West – with much fewer Health Act partnerships in the London, South East and Eastern regions.
- Only one partnership included a local authority department outside of social services (education), with the vast majority of partnerships remaining the sole preserve of the NHS and SSDs.

- The most common type of partnership was a pooled budget (80% of respondents), followed by integrated provision (46%) and lead commissioning (6%).
- Partnerships covered a wide range of user groups, including older people (50% of respondents), people with learning difficulties (41%), people with a physical impairment (23%) and adults with mental health problems (14%).
- Partnerships covered a wide range of services, including residential/ nursing/respite care (41% of respondents), community/continuing care (36%), day care (32%) and intermediate care/rehabilitation (32%).
- Although more than £200 million was being invested in 2000–2001 in the 20 partnerships that provided financial data, there were substantial variations, with approximately one-third of partnerships investing more than £10 million, but with 40% investing sums of £500 000 or less. This led the researchers to comment that 'the flexibilities may be seen in these cases as a "bolt on" initiative rather than a re-orientation of the way mainstream business is done' (p. 42).
- Charging raised something of a dilemma, with 55% of partnerships responding having decided to charge for the social care element of their work and 46% not doing so.
- Despite difficulties in assessing the data, the involvement of the independent sector and of users and carers appeared to be relatively low.
- There were substantial levels of joint training and information-sharing with regard to issues such as clients, finance and service activity.
- Although the respondents were generally positive about local partnerships, they identified key problems, such as the organisational practicalities that partnership working can generate, rather than concerns to do with overall vision.

Overall, the Health Act seems to have offered participating agencies considerable freedom in order to develop new ways of working with regard to a range of services and a range of user groups. The apparent progress that participating agencies have made with regard to joint training and information sharing is also to be welcomed, whereas the substantial sums that some agencies have invested in new partnerships is perhaps an indication of their commitment to working more effectively together. Despite this, the small number of partnerships making early use of their new powers is disappointing and may mean that only those agencies with a good history of joint working were included in the interim report of the national evaluation. Although it is difficult to be certain at this stage, there is a danger that the discretionary nature of the reforms may only appeal to those who are already working well together, failing to be taken up by those who, arguably, need them the most – those organisations that have a poor track record of joint working and who may require a more mandatory approach before they collaborate. Certainly this is a view that has been expressed by the current author in a number of commentaries:

> There is considerable danger that the Government's proposals will lead to a two-tier system, in which progressive authorities are enabled to provide services on a much more integrated basis while those agencies struggling to collaborate with local health providers will fall increasingly behind. (Glasby 2000c, p. 12)

> Crucially, [the Health Act powers] were not mandatory ... Whilst the Partnership in Action proposals would enable some authorities to work together more creatively, therefore, they did not tackle the root cause of the problem. With discretionary measures such as this, the danger was always that those authorities who had worked well together in the past would use their new flexibilities to collaborate even more closely. In contrast, those who had a history of mutual distrust and recriminations would continue to operate in isolation from each other, becoming increasingly distanced from their more progressive colleagues. (Glasby, forthcoming)

Similar concerns may also be apparent within government itself, which has frequently expressed its frustration at the lack of progress in improving partnership working, leading to ongoing speculation as to precisely what the future may hold for health and social care (*see*, for example, Community Care 2000; Huber 2000; Winchester 2000). As a result, there have been a number of hints that the government may wish to intervene in order to compel local agencies to enter into partnership arrangements – surely an indication that the discretionary nature of the original *Partnership in Action* initiative was misplaced.

Further limitations of the Health Act 'flexibilities' include the somewhat unconvincing statement that major structural upheaval should be avoided as a tactic that would be too disruptive and expensive. Whereas widespread change may be traumatic, fear of upheaval, ultimately, is not a good enough reason for failing to adopt a strategic, long-term solution to the difficulties of joint working which may well need to involve considerable organisational reform. Also of concern is the suggestion cited above that some of the Health Act partnerships may be a 'bolt on' to current services rather than a more fundamental attempt to change the way that partner organisations operate. If this is repeated elsewhere as the Health Act is implemented more widely, there is a danger that partnership working may become little more than a 'token gesture' – something that many agencies do, but not an activity that shapes their everyday work or core business. Overall, therefore, the *Partnership in Action* initiative seems likely to improve joint working in some areas of the country and enables participating agencies to work together in new and more flexible ways. Despite this, the policy falls short of the more fundamental changes required to resolve the difficulties associated with the hospital discharge of older people and the health–social care divide.

Intermediate care

Intermediate care is a concept that has developed against the background of a series of increasing and interconnected pressures on health and social services.

- There has been a long-term increase in acute and general hospital admissions per head of approximately 3.5% per annum (Department of Health 2000b, p. 5). Although rising admissions are particularly problematic during the winter months, there is evidence that substantial pressures on hospital beds can occur at any time of the year (Moore 1995; NHS Confederation 1997).
- Rising admissions have been offset by reductions in the length of hospital stays. From 1981 to 1996/97 average acute length of stay (per finished consultant episode) decreased from 9.3 to 5.0 days, whereas average geriatric stays fell from 66.1 to 18.6 days (Vaughan and Lathlean 1999, p. 3). This has meant that those entering hospital for acute medical treatment are now being discharged much more quickly than was once thought possible or desirable, placing greater pressure on community services (Glasby and Littlechild 2000b).
- The lack of alternative facilities means that some people are inappropriately admitted to hospital, remain in acute care beds longer than is necessary and are prematurely placed in long-stay residential or nursing care (*see*, for example, Department of Health 2000b; Glasby and Littlechild 2000b).
- Demographic changes mean that there are a growing number of older people who may require support from health and social services. Since 1931 the number of older people has doubled, and the number of people aged 85 and over is expected to triple between the late 1990s and 2050 (Royal Commission on Long Term Care 1999).

In seeking to come to terms with such pressures, there have been a number of key responses from the government:

- the promotion of independence as a key goal for community care services
- the development of intermediate care services to prevent unnecessary hospital admissions, facilitate effective discharge and prevent unnecessary long-term admissions to residential or nursing care.

Promoting independence

Since New Labour came into office in May 1997, the promotion of independence and the prevention of unnecessary admissions to hospital or to long-stay residential or nursing care have become key features of health and social care for older people and other adult user groups. Key policies have included:

- a Better Services for Vulnerable People initiative to optimise independence through timely recuperation and rehabilitation opportunities (Department of Health 1997c)
- emphasis on promoting independence in national priorities guidance (Department of Health 1998c)
- new specific grants to encourage a focus on prevention and independence (Department of Health 2000c, 2001j)
- a national strategy for carers (Department of Health 2000d)
- emphasis on rehabilitation and on preventing premature admissions to residential or nursing care in the document produced by the Royal Commission on Long Term Care (1999)
- the extension of direct payments to older people, carers and younger disabled people (Department of Health 1998b, 2001k).

Measures to promote independence have also been advocated by the Audit Commission (1997, 2000), which has identified a 'vicious circle' in health and social care (*see* Figure 6.1). As the number of hospital admissions rises, lengths of hospital stay decline, opportunities for rehabilitation are reduced, there is an increased use of expensive residential or nursing home care and less money for preventative services, thereby leading to more hospital admissions.

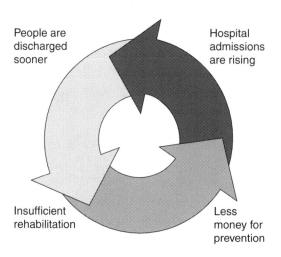

Pressures on hospital beds are increasing

People are discharged sooner

Hospital admissions are rising

Insufficient rehabilitation

Less money for prevention

Increasing use of expensive residential or nursing care

Figure 6.1 The 'vicious circle'.

Intermediate care

Against this background, the development of intermediate care services is one means of breaking out of the Audit Commission's 'vicious circle' and delivering on the government's commitment to joint working, prevention and promoting independence. In February 2000, the National Beds Inquiry outlined three possible scenarios for the future of hospital services (Department of Health 2000b):

- *Maintaining the current direction*: retaining the current balance between hospital and community services, with a slight rise in bed capacity in the acute sector.
- *Acute bed-focused care*: an active policy to increase the number of hospital beds and concentrate services in acute care.
- *Care closer to home*: an expansion of community services and the development of intermediate care (services designed to prevent avoidable admissions to acute care and facilitate the transition from hospital to home and from medical dependence to functional independence).

When the response to the Inquiry was published, there was overwhelming support for the 'care closer to home' option and for greater partnership working between health and social care (Department of Health n.d.).

In July 2000 *The NHS Plan* (Department of Health 2000a) announced an extra £900 million to be invested over four years in intermediate care services, such as rapid response teams, intensive rehabilitation services, recuperation facilities, one-stop shops and integrated home care teams. *The NHS Plan* set clear targets for the expansion of intermediate care and was followed by shorter-term milestones in *The NHS Plan Implementation Programme* (Department of Health 2000e) (*see* Appendix B).

In January 2001 government guidance provided more detail about how intermediate care would operate (Department of Health 2001e). According to circular 2001/001, intermediate care should be regarded as describing services that meet *all* the following criteria (Department of Health 2001e, p. 6):

- are targeted at people who would otherwise face unnecessarily prolonged hospital stays or inappropriate admission to acute inpatient care, long-term residential care or continuing NHS inpatient care
- are provided on the basis of a comprehensive assessment, resulting in a structured individual care plan that involves active therapy, treatment or opportunity for recovery
- have a planned outcome of maximising independence and typically enabling patients or users to resume living at home
- are time-limited, normally no longer than six weeks and frequently as little as one or two weeks or less

- involve cross-professional working, with a single assessment framework, single professional records and shared protocols.

In particular, intermediate care should be distinguished from:

- transitional care that does not involve active therapy or other interventions to maximise independence (e.g. for patients ready to leave acute inpatient care and waiting for longer-term packages of care to be arranged)
- longer-term rehabilitation or support services
- rehabilitation that forms part of acute hospital care.

In order to offer users and carers a seamless service, the NHS and councils should make optimum use of pooled budgets, other Health Act 'flexibilities' and the developing Care Trust model. Crucially, additional NHS resources for intermediate care will be available subject to resources being deployed as part of pooled funds under the Health Act 'flexibilities' from 2001–02.* Intermediate care services should also be provided to patients free of charge and should generally be located in community-based settings or in patients' own homes. The NHS and councils should ensure that systems for evaluating intermediate care services are built in from the earliest possible stage of planning and implementation. They should also consult and take into account the views of *patients or users and carers* on current patterns of service delivery and on the potential effect of developing new intermediate care services [emphasis in the original]. Throughout, the NHS and local authorities should take into account the potential contribution of the independent sector and, where appropriate, develop services in partnership with independent providers.

In March 2001, Standard Three of the *National Service Framework for Older People* specified that (Department of Health 2001m, p. 41):

> Older people will have access to a new range of intermediate care services at home or in designated care settings, to promote their independence by providing enhanced services from the NHS and councils to prevent unnecessary hospital admission and effective rehabilitation services to enable early discharge from hospital and to prevent premature or unnecessary admission to long-term residential care.

In particular, intermediate care services should focus on three key areas:

1 responding to, or averting, crises through information and advice services, intensive support at home and step-up care in residential or other settings

---

*In practice, this requirement does not appear to have been enforced, since additional funding for intermediate care is hypothecated rather than ringfenced.

2 active rehabilitation following an acute hospital stay to maximise independence and prevent readmission to hospital or premature admission to long-term care

3 preventing inappropriate admissions to long-term residential or nursing home care.

Intermediate care services will include medical, nursing, therapy and social work involvement, and will use an integrated multi-professional record. Partnership with the independent sector should be actively sought and links with community equipment and housing improvement will be essential. More recently, the government's emphasis on the importance of intermediate care has been demonstrated by a number of further developments, as follows.

- In March 2001, the Secretary of State for Health published national minimum standards for care homes for older people under section 23(1) of the Care Standards Act 2000 (Department of Health 2001n). These standards apply to all homes for which registration as care homes is required (including intermediate care facilities) and came into force from 1 April 2002, unless otherwise stated in any standard (*see* Appendix B).
- The government launched a guide to contracting with the independent sector and a series of model contracts for residential, day and domiciliary intermediate care services (Department of Health 2001o).
- As an indication of the government's commitment to intermediate care, the Department of Health announced a new award scheme for excellence in intermediate care, launched to coincide with the 101st birthday of the Queen Mother (Department of Health 2001p).
- The provision of capital funding worth £66 million over two years to support the development of intermediate care (Department of Health 2001q). Under this scheme, Regional Offices were to submit prioritised bids for their regions by 11 January 2002, for funding to be approved by ministers.
- The creation of a series of pilot projects in order to explore the potential contribution of the voluntary sector to intermediate care (Help the Aged 2001).
- The commissioning of a number of formal evaluations of intermediate care services.

Potential impact

Of all the policy initiatives described in this book, intermediate care has by far the largest potential to improve hospital discharge practices. If handled correctly, there is clearly scope for intermediate care schemes to engage in a range of activities that will improve the care of older people and facilitate swift and effective discharge. Examples might include hospital at home schemes, discharge co-ordination initiatives, improved rehabilitation and convalescence services and projects to prevent the need for hospital care altogether (*see* Vaughan and Lathlean (1999) for further examples). At face value, intermediate care is such a common-sense concept that it is difficult to fault the current emphasis on developing such services (*see* Box 6.3).

Box 6.3   Intermediate care

You're 90, live alone and have a fall. Your hip cracks, you're taken to hospital. While you're there you get a chest infection, then pneumonia. The pneumonia is brought under control but you are still weak, and the broken hip has exacerbated mobility problems caused by arthritis. Acute beds are under pressure, so you are assessed and found a bed in a residential home. You never go home again.

Intermediate care should rewrite this story. Instead of being taken to hospital, you could perhaps expect to receive an intensive 'hospital at home' service, followed by a multi-disciplinary planned rehabilitation programme. If you needed to be admitted to an acute bed, you could be discharged to a residential intermediate care facility, perhaps based in a nursing home, for a six-week programme of physiotherapy, occupational therapy, medical and nursing care and social work support. Either way, at least in theory, you end up back in your own home instead of living out your days in an institution.

Source: Rickford 2001, p. 18

Despite this, it is not clear whether intermediate care will be sufficient to resolve the deep-seated problems outlined above with regard to the hospital discharge of older people. Although definitive evidence remains scarce until recently commissioned evaluations begin to report, key limitations of intermediate care are thought to include (*see*, for example, Glasby 2001b, 2001c; Goodwin 2002; Rickford 2001; Vaughan and Lathlean 1999):

- a lack of awareness of roles and responsibilities in other services
- the segregated nature of current professional education, which prevents greater understanding of each other's role and function
- the lack of co-terminous boundaries between services
- the difficulty of integrating small-scale winter pressures projects into mainstream service provision

- concerns that the NHS and SSDs have not spent all the money they have received for intermediate care on the purpose for which it was intended, using it to make up for shortfalls in other services.

Some of these tensions can be illustrated in more detail via a case study based on the development of a business plan for an intermediate care facility in the West Midlands. Although this has been described in more detail elsewhere (Glasby 2002b), the business plan revealed a number of difficulties that front-line agencies may face in trying to deliver the government's intermediate care agenda:

- *Different professional values held by key stakeholders*: in drawing up a multi-agency business plan, different professionals and agencies had different attitudes towards a range of issues, including the balance between professional power and user choice, and between security and calculated risk-taking by service users.
- *Different organisational agendas*: whereas several GPs were concerned that the proposed intermediate care facility was located close to their surgeries, the local hospital wished the service to be based in one of its own under-utilised buildings. In contrast, the SSD wanted to run the service from a former residential home and to be selected as the chosen provider.
- *The lack of co-terminous boundaries between partner agencies*: drawing up the business plan involved contributions from primary care, secondary care, social care, housing and the independent sector, many of whom covered different geographical areas. As a result, local partners had to work in partnership not only with each other, but also with PCGs, SSDs and hospitals outside the local area.
- *The need to overcome significant organisational upheavals within individual partner agencies*: the business plan was compiled at a time when local PCGs were in the process of becoming PCTs, a local hospital was merging with a nearby hospital and the SSD was being reorganised.
- *Financial confusion*: some local health and social care agencies may be uncertain where the 'new' money pledged by central government has gone, how much money has been received and how much is actually available. In some areas, it is possible that the 'new' money may not be specifically set aside for intermediate care, but simply incorporated into the annual budget or used to compensate for shortfalls elsewhere in the system. In this particular case study, a significant proportion of the government's new money had already been spent in reducing previous overspends and taking account of inflation. With no additional money available, the business plan had to identify existing projects that could be incorporated into the proposed intermediate care facility, redirecting existing resources into the new service. Hardly surprisingly, this created

significant tensions amongst local agencies and meant that the project was under considerable financial pressure before it had even begun.
- *The difficulty of establishing new services that span traditional boundaries within tight timescales.*

Additional concerns about the capacity of intermediate care to resolve current concerns about hospital discharge have also been raised by the House of Commons Health Committee (2002, pp. 27–32). Key issues include:

- a lack of clarity about what the term 'intermediate' care means
- the difficulty of achieving a strategic and integrated care system
- a tendency to focus on providing 'more beds' rather than on reconfiguring existing services to invest more heavily in community services
- inappropriate placements in some intermediate care schemes
- fears that additional government money had been 'siphoned off' for other purposes
- a lack of commitment to working in partnership with the independent sector
- a tendency to 're-badge' existing services as intermediate care rather than develop new initiatives
- the emphasis of government guidance on a six-week timescale rather than on working at the pace of the individual older person.

Summary

Since 1997, the New Labour government has introduced a number of policy initiatives that have the potential to revolutionise the way in which health and social services work together. Under the three policies reviewed above, there have been a number of key advances:

- additional funding to help health and social services cope with winter pressures has enabled local partners to develop new projects to improve joint working and to facilitate prompt and effective discharges from hospital
- new legislation has begun to remove previous barriers to effective joint working, enabling health and social care agencies to work together in more flexible, imaginative ways
- new investment in intermediate care has the potential to create new health and social care services that prevent people from being admitted to hospital unnecessarily, facilitate swift discharge and aid rehabilitation and recovery.

Despite this, each policy has a number of key limitations:

- Short-term, non-recurrent funding is not sufficient to resolve long-term and deep-seated problems. As a result, many effective schemes ceased to function and were not able to make a permanent impact upon mainstream services and practice. Injecting sudden sums of money into the health and social care system can also store up trouble for the future, leaving agencies with ongoing financial commitments after the initial funding has ceased.
- Discretionary powers to work together in new ways are more likely to benefit those agencies who already work well together, leaving agencies with a poor history of partnership working further and further behind. Some Health Act partnerships may also be more of a 'bolt on' to existing services rather than a fundamental attempt to change the way in which local agencies collaborate.
- Intermediate care services have the potential to span traditional service boundaries, but do not change the fact that those boundaries will continue to exist. Thus, intermediate care seems likely to be beset by the many of the same difficulties as previous attempts to improve joint working – different boundaries, professional values, funding streams and priorities – without necessarily providing the means to overcome such obstacles.

Against this background, it seems unlikely that any of the developments described above will provide a definitive solution to the significant difficulties associated with the hospital discharge of older people. At an individual and organisational level, New Labour policies may be seen to have contributed to the development of new services, promoted joint training and enabled local agencies to work together more flexibly. Despite blurring the boundaries of existing services in several important respects, however, none of these achievements have been able to eradicate the structural barriers to joint working and many obstacles remain. As a result, it may be that even more profound changes are required if the policy and practice issues highlighted in this book are to be overcome (*see* Chapter 7 for a further discussion).

Conclusion

By way of conclusion, this chapter revisits four statements highlighted during the overview of research presented earlier in the book (Chapters 4 and 5). In the first of the four quotes below, Henwood and Wistow (1993) identify a central tension between two competing notions of good practice with regard to hospital discharge. Although hospital services are often underpinned by a resource management model that seeks to make cost-effective use of scarce resources and maximise the throughput of patients, SSDs adopt a more user-centred model which emphasises individual choice and needs-led assessment. In the second quotation, the House of Commons Select Committee on Public Accounts (2001) cites comments by the NHS Executive about the financial and political barriers to promoting closer joint working between health and social care and reducing the number of delayed discharges. In the third and fourth quotations, the House of Commons Health Committee (1999, 2002) calls for integrated health and social services in order to end the current fragmentation, confusion and duplication experienced by service users and their carers.

> There were conflicting perspectives on what constituted success in hospital discharge. The principal tension, which was observed to a lesser or greater extent in all localities, was between a narrowly defined resource management model, and one which might be described as user-centred. We would argue that a definition of success needs to encompass elements of both perspectives. Discharges need to be timely, and should not be delayed unnecessarily, but should also be undertaken at the pace which best suits the needs and wishes of the individual. This synthesis of perspectives requires a greater degree of change within the approach currently dominated by resource efficiency concerns. For the acute hospital sector in particular this will require a substantial cultural change, and the development of a more holistic approach towards the care of individuals. This also requires an awareness of outcomes which are not defined solely in terms of processes or service activity levels, but in terms of the quality of life for the individual concerned. (Henwood and Wistow 1993, pp. 36–37)

> The [NHS] Executive assured us that the partnership between the Health Service and Social Services had improved enormously. There was a seam between the services, and there was a need for an integrated health and social services system that worked for patients ... While the Executive were trying to integrate the services, the system did nevertheless operate with two cheque books, and local government had other legitimate priorities that might affect social care budgets. There were variations around the country in where the lines were drawn between

health and social care. The Executive could lay down some ground rules, for example that avoided conflict between health authorities and local authorities over who was going to fund a daily visit to someone to help them bathe properly and get dressed. But a more fundamental redrawing of the boundary between health and social care was complex and political. (House of Commons Select Committee on Public Accounts 2001, para. 44–45)

We consider the current system for continuing health and social care to be very confused. Responsibilities are blurred, professionals face unnecessary problems, and users and carers are suffering because of barriers created by a structural division which is based on an ill-defined and arguably non-existent boundary. We commend all those who have tried to establish seamless care for users and carers despite these barriers. They have shown levels of personal commitment and determination which we regard as admirable ... **However we consider that the problems of collaboration between health and social services will not be properly resolved until there is an integrated health and social care system, whether this is within the NHS, within local government or within some new, separate organisation. We acknowledge that such an integration would lead to an emphasis on the boundary between the health and social care body and other functions, for instance housing and education, but we believe that it is the only sensible long term solution to end the current confusion.** (House of Commons Health Committee 1999, p. xviii [emphasis in the original])

The evidence we have heard simply strengthens our view, stated in our predecessor Committee's inquiry into the relationship between health and social services ..., that the problems of collaboration between health and social services will not be properly resolved until there is an integrated health and social care system, whether this is in the NHS, within local government or within some new separate organisation. We recognise that [recent government initiatives] all add to the incentives for health and local authorities to work together, but they fall short of unifying the two agencies ... For many years there has been insistent exhortation for these bodies to work together. Unless there is a rapid change and clear evidence that the challenges of delayed discharges are being effectively managed by joint working, it will be further proof that leads to the inescapable conclusion that radical structural reform is required. (House of Commons Health Committee 2002, p. 58)

In Chapters 2 and 3 of this book, we have seen how welfare services in the UK have been dominated by an ongoing belief in the feasibility of distinguishing between health and social care needs. Although definitions of health and social care are contested and have changed over time, the contemporary welfare system is still based on this division, with separate services responsible for separate aspects of service users or patients' needs. This has acquired increasing significance following the community care reforms of the early 1990s, with hospitals much more dependent upon the assessment and care management role of local authority SSDs in order to discharge patients from hospital to community services. Because of the imperative to control rapidly increasing public expenditure, moreover, we have also seen how SSDs were likely to face substantial financial difficulties as the new system began to bed down.

Against this background, many of the policy initiatives summarised in Chapters 2 and 3 were insufficient to tackle a problem as longstanding and as deep-seated as hospital discharge and joint working between health and social care. Often, central government left hospital discharge to local discretion, issuing guidance which compelled local agencies to negotiate their own policies and procedures. Where central policy documents referred to hospital discharge at all, the emphasis was on good practice guidance and on exhortations to further collaboration, without tackling the underlying barriers to more effective joint working. Throughout, there has been an ongoing failure to recognise that the problematic nature of hospital discharge is not necessarily the fault of individual workers or agencies, but rather the product of much more fundamental and structural obstacles embedded in a system based on a rigid but highly debatable demarcation between health and social care.

As a result of the failure of central government to 'grasp the bull by the horns' and take decisive, long-term action to resolve the issues at stake, research over more than 30 years has continually emphasised the same key findings (*see* Chapters 4 and 5):

- failure to give patients and their carers adequate notice of discharge
- failure to involve patients and their carers in decisions about discharge and ongoing care arrangements
- failure of health and social care practitioners to work effectively together
- hospital-based delays in arranging transport or medication
- failure of health and social care practitioners to work effectively together
- the incompatibility of two different systems based on different notions of good practice
- lack of attention to the needs of carers
- the problematic nature of hospital discharge for other user groups and throughout the UK
- structural barriers, such as separate funding streams, and the need to overcome a range of organisational and professional boundaries in order to achieve seamless services.

Under the New Labour government elected in 1997, a number of more recent initiatives have sought to improve inter-agency collaboration through mechanisms such as winter pressures monies, Health Act 'flexibilities' and intermediate care (*see* Chapter 6). Although these measures represent an important step forward, they share many of the limitations of previous government policies during the early and mid-1990s:

- an emphasis on local discretion when seeking to improve joint working
- short- rather than long-term solutions
- the failure to give sufficient weight to the underlying structural barriers to partnership working.

As a result, it seems unlikely that New Labour will prove any more successful than its predecessors in resolving the longstanding difficulties associated with hospital discharge.

At various stages in this book, the problematic nature of hospital discharge has been summarised in terms of three overlapping areas of activity: individual, organisational and structural (*see* Figure 7.1).

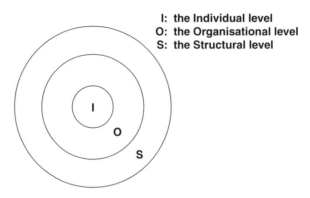

Figure 7.1 Understanding partnership working in health and social care. (Adapted from Glasby 2000b, 2002c; Thompson 2001.)

The benefit of such a representation is that it emphasises the complex interplay of the many factors that help to shape hospital discharge practices in the UK. Thus, the contribution of individuals, though significant, takes place within an organisational context, which itself is influenced by structural barriers to improved joint working. Similarly, structural barriers derive at least in part from certain organisational features associated with particular types of health and social care agency and, ultimately, from the individual practitioners working within the organisations concerned. Crucially, however, the model also provides a framework for formulating possible policy responses to tackle the problems associated with hospital discharge and with partnership working more generally. Although it is beyond the scope of this book to present a detailed agenda for change, some preliminary ideas are set out below:

- At an *individual level* action is required to improve the way in which individual practitioners work with older people, communicate with patients and carers, and collaborate with each other. Possible policies to consider at this level include joint training and a greater emphasis on interpersonal skills such as empathy and communication skills during pre- and post-qualifying education.

- At an *organisational level* local health and social care agencies have a responsibility to ensure that they work with partner organisations to achieve the best possible outcomes for users and carers. At this level, therefore, previous policies have been right to identify the need for jointly agreed hospital discharge procedures, to promote good practice and to encourage agencies to develop flexible responses at a local level.
- At a *structural level*, however, there remains a need for much more concerted action to eradicate the underlying financial, legal, political and administrative barriers to partnership working. As the four quotes at the start of this chapter highlight, hospital discharge is beset by competing notions of good practice among health and social care agencies and a range of structural divisions which mitigate against the co-ordinated provision of health and social care. In the opinion of the House of Commons Health Committee (1999, 2002), these divisions cannot be resolved until there is an integrated health and social care system in place, providing service users and patients with the support they need irrespective of whether it would traditionally have been delivered by a nurse from the NHS or a home carer from the SSD. This is an opinion that is shared by the current author, who agrees that major structural change is the only way to achieve successful partnership working and to improve the experiences of older people and other service users discharged from NHS hospitals to health and social care in the community. Integrated services would mean that there was one agency responsible for both health and social care and that there were fewer vested interests involved in the discharge process. Integrated health and social care would also mean that more strategic and long-term decisions could be taken about service provision and about the care of individual patients, providing more of an holistic response and enabling money to be spent as appropriately as possible. Thus, the management team of an integrated service would not wish to discharge a patient prematurely in order to free up a hospital bed, or delay a discharge unnecessarily so that they would not have to meet the cost of someone's care package in the community. Instead, an integrated service would be able to decide what the person's needs were and where the best place would be to meet those needs, without the temptation of 'passing the buck' to another agency in order to protect its budget. Crucially, integrated services would lead to more co-ordinated care for patients and prevent many of the blockages currently experienced by the NHS. Ultimately, the only way to provide truly 'seamless services' is surely to remove the seam altogether.

Of course, structural change on its own is not the answer, and we have already seen how integrated services in Northern Ireland have not been sufficient to secure fully satisfactory hospital discharges (Chapter 5). Indeed, by itself action at any one level alone is probably bound to fail. By developing policies to tackle the individual, organisational and structural aspects of hospital discharge, however, there is a possibility that we might be able to understand the issues at stake more fully and finally begin to resolve them.

Methodological issues

Although Chapters 4 and 5 of this book have identified a number of key research findings with regard to the hospital discharge of older people, our understanding of the issues at stake is sometimes clouded by a number of methodological concerns. Whereas the consistency of the evidence cited above provides a satisfactory overview of the key problems and themes, it is important to remember that current approaches to researching and monitoring hospital discharge are not without their problems. In particular, there are three main issues to consider (all of which tend to be true of research into delayed discharges as well as research into inappropriate hospital admissions – topics which have both been approached in similar ways).

1 Traditionally, many researchers have adopted extremely subjective approaches to the topic in question, labelling days of care as appropriate or inappropriate either on the basis of their own opinion or with reference to some sort of expert panel of medical practitioners. Unfortunately, such inherent subjectivity makes it very difficult to compare results with findings elsewhere, and some studies are unclear as to whether they are measuring the number of people who, in an ideal situation, could be cared for in alternative settings or those inappropriately placed within the context of existing local services. There is also evidence to suggest that results vary according to the seniority and/or professional background of the 'expert' being asked to assess 'appropriateness' (*see*, for example, Bartlett *et al.* 1999; McCulloch *et al.* 1997; McDonagh *et al.* 2000).

2 More recently, researchers have sought to develop more rigorous and objective methods of assessing the extent of inappropriate admissions and delayed discharges in different hospitals in different areas of the country. Often, this has revolved around the use of clinical review instruments – standardised lists of criteria, usually relating to the severity of a patient's condition and the type and intensity of service provided. If a specified number of these criteria are satisfied, the patient is considered to be appropriately located in hospital. Examples of instruments used in recent British studies include the Intensity–Severity–Discharge Review System with Adult Criteria (Coast *et al.* 1995, 1996a, 1996b), the Appropriateness Evaluation Protocol (Gertman and Restuccia 1981) and

the Oxford Bed Study Instrument (Anderson *et al.* 1988) (*see also* Box A.1 for a practical example). Although these instruments produce easily quantifiable results and reduce the inherent subjectivity of previous methodologies, they have a number of limitations when used in isolation (*see* Glasby and Littlechild 2000b, 2001; Littlechild and Glasby 2000, 2001; McDonagh *et al.* 2000 for a more detailed discussion):

- clinical review instruments are often applied as if in a 'vacuum' and take no account of local circumstances or the availability of alternative services
- researchers applying clinical review instruments do so retrospectively and therefore enjoy the benefit of hindsight
- some clinical review instruments are not as reliable or as valid as is sometimes suggested, frequently overestimating the number of inappropriate admissions or days of care (Strumwasser *et al.* 1990)
- on their own, review instruments simply classify admissions or days of care as appropriate or inappropriate. This is only half the story, and more detailed research is required to answer more significant questions such as why those admissions or days of care deemed inappropriate took place in the first place and how they could have been prevented
- some tools exclude specific groups of people, such as children or those with mental health problems
- how instruments are applied can influence the results (for example, whether they are applied concurrently or retrospectively, to a cross-sectional sample of days or to entire hospital stays for a sample of patients, etc.).

3 Above all, however, many attempts to assess the rate of inappropriate admission and delayed discharges have tended to be quantitative in nature and have been dominated by research and/or health professionals. Thus, the 'expert opinion' studies outlined above rely heavily on the opinion of the individual researcher or a wider body of experts, whereas clinical review instruments are administered to a patient's case notes by medical and research professionals without considering the potential input of the individual patient. Patients are often experts in their own condition and can make a useful contribution to understanding how and why an admission came to take place or how a discharge came to be delayed. This contextual information can be crucial, offering researchers an insight into the events leading up to the admission or discharge and providing a much more holistic view than simply analysing medical notes and administering a review instrument.

Box A.1 The Oxford Bed Study Instrument

A patient is considered to have a positive reason for being in hospital if one of the following criteria is met:

- has that day a life-threatening condition that requires treatment or observation, including acute haematological disorders
- any invasive therapeutic or investigative procedure that day
- post-operative day for the above criterion
- requiring close medical monitoring by a doctor
- undergoing ventilation
- undergoing any form of intravenous therapy
- care of major surgical wound and drainage
- continuous monitoring of vital signs, including cardiac monitoring
- scheduled for any invasive therapeutic or investigative procedure or requiring pre-operative evaluation

Source: Anderson *et al.* 1988

Additional concerns have also been raised by the House of Commons Health Committee (2002), which has questioned the accuracy of official monitoring figures. Key issues include:

- a lack of reliable figures for delayed discharges in community hospitals as opposed to acute care
- local differences in interpretation
- confusion as to whether to count delays in terms of the number of days or the number of working days
- confusion about whether to count patients delayed for less than eight days
- the emphasis on the delayed discharges of older people (aged over 75), which may mask the true extent of the problem.

As a result of these concerns, the House of Commons Health Committee has called for further clarification and refinement of official data collection processes so as to improve our knowledge of the extent of delayed hospital discharges.

APPENDIX B

Key milestones for intermediate care

During 2000–2001, health and social services should:

- ensure that there are 1500 more intermediate care beds in 2001–2002 compared with 1999–2000
- ensure that 60 000 more people receive intermediate care services in 2001–2002 compared with 1999–2000
- ensure that 25 000 more carers benefit from respite or breaks services in 2001–2002 compared with 2000–2001
- ensure that the number of older people helped to live at home per 1000 of the population aged 65 or over increases by at least 2% nationally in 2001–2002 compared with 2000–2001.

Meeting these targets will achieve in 2001–2002:

- an average rate of delayed transfer of care of 10% for people aged 75 and over
- a reduction of an average of approximately 1000 hospital beds occupied at any time by people aged 75 and over awaiting transfer of care when compared with 2000–2001
- an increase in the per capita rate of emergency admissions for people aged 75 and over of less than 2% when compared with 2000–2001
- no increase in the rate of emergency readmissions within 28 days of discharge when compared with 2000–2001.

By 2004, there will be:

- 5000 extra intermediate care and 1700 supported intermediate care places together benefiting approximately 150 000 more older people each year
- rapid response teams and other avoidable admission prevention schemes benefiting approximately 70 000 more people each year
- 50 000 more people enabled to live at home through additional home care and other support
- carers' respite services extended to benefit a further 75 000 carers and those they care for.

(*Sources*: Department of Health 2000a, 2000e, 2001m.)

National minimum standards for care homes for older people also include a specific reference to intermediate care (Department of Health 2001n, pp. 5–6):

Standard 6: Service users assessed and referred solely for intermediate care are helped to maximise their independence and return home.

6.1 **Where service users are admitted only for intermediate care, dedicated accommodation is provided, together with specialised facilities, equipment and staff, to deliver short term intensive rehabilitation and enable service users to return home.**

6.2 Rehabilitation facilities are sited in dedicated space and include equipment for therapies and rehabilitation, as well as equipment to promote activities of daily living.

6.3 Staff are qualified and/or are trained and appropriately supervised to use techniques for rehabilitation including treatment and recovery programmes, promotion of mobility, continence and self-care, and outreach programmes to re-establish community living.

6.4 Staff are deployed and specialist services from relevant professionals including occupational and physiotherapists are provided or secured in sufficient numbers and with sufficient competence and skills, to meet the assessed needs of service users admitted for rehabilitation.

6.5 The service user placed for intermediate care is not admitted for long term care unless and until the requirements regarding information, assessment and care planning are met.*

---

*That is, prospective service users have the information they need to make an informed choice about where to live, no service user moves into the home without having their needs assessed and being assured that these will be met and the user's health, personal and social care needs are set out in an individual plan of care.

References

- Adams S (2001) *On the Mend? Hospital Discharge Services and the Role of Home Improvement Agencies*. London, Care and Repair England.
- Age Concern Liverpool (1975) *Going Home? The Care of Elderly Patients after Discharge from Hospital* (Report on the Continuing Care Project). Liverpool, Age Concern Liverpool.
- Anderson P, Meara J, Broadhurst S, Attwood S, Timbrell M and Gatherer A (1988) Use of hospital beds: a cohort study of admissions to a provincial teaching hospital. *British Medical Journal* **297**: 910–912.
- Anderson Report (1947) *The Care and Treatment of the Elderly and Infirm*. London, British Medical Association.
- Andrews C and Wilson T (1953) Organisation of a geriatric service in a rural area. *Lancet*, 18 April, 785–789.
- Arskey H, Heaton J and Sloper P (1997) *Carers' Perspectives on Hospital Discharge Procedures for Young Adults with Physical and Complex Disabilities*. York, Social Policy Research Unit.
- Audit Commission (1986) *Making a Reality of Community Care*. London, HMSO.
- Audit Commission (1992*) Lying in Wait: the use of medical beds in acute hospitals*. London, HMSO.
- Audit Commission (1997) *The Coming of Age: improving care services for older people*. London, Audit Commission.
- Audit Commission (2000) *The Way to Go Home: rehabilitation and remedial services for older people*. London, Audit Commission.
- Baggott R (1998) *Health and Health Care in Britain* (2e). Basingstoke, Macmillan.
- Ballinger BR, Ballinger CB, Reid AH and McQueen E (1991) The psychiatric symptoms, diagnosis and care needs of 100 mentally handicapped patients. *British Journal of Psychiatry* **158**: 251–254.
- Barnes M (1997) *Care, Communities and Citizens*. London, Longman.
- Barnes M and Bennett G (1998) Frail bodies, courageous voices: older people influencing community care. *Health and Social Care in the Community* **6**: 102–111.
- Barnes M and Bennett-Emslie G (1997) *'If They would Listen …': an evaluation of the Fife User Panels*. Edinburgh, Age Concern Scotland.
- Barnes M and Cormie J (1995) On the panel. *Health Service Journal*, 2 March, 30–31.
- Barnes M, Cormie J and Crichton M (1994) *Seeking Representative Views from Frail Older People*. Edinburgh, Age Concern Scotland.
- Bartlett C, Holloway J, Evans M and Harrison G (1999) Projection of alternatives to acute psychiatric beds: review of an emerging service assessment method. *Journal of Mental Health* **8**: 555–568.
- BBC (1994) *Panorama: the greatest nightmare*. London, BBC.

- Bebbington A and Tong M (1986) Trends and changes in old people's homes: provision over twenty years. In: K Judge and I Sinclair (eds) *Residential Care for Elderly People: research contributions to the development of policy and practice*. London, HMSO.
- *Birmingham Evening Mail* (2001) It's not good enough, Mr Milburn: what we need are real answers. *Birmingham Evening Mail*, 28 June, 1.
- Boucher Report (1957) *Survey of Services Available to the Chronic Sick and Elderly 1945–55* (Reports on Public Health and Medical Subjects No. 98). London, HMSO.
- Bradshaw J (1988) Financing private care for the elderly. In: S Baldwin, G Parker and R Walker (eds) *Social Security and Community Care*. Aldershot, Avebury.
- British Medical Association (1948) *The Right Patient in the Right Bed*. First Supplement to the Report of the Committee on the Care and Treatment of the Elderly and Infirm. London, BMA.
- Burstow P (n.d.) *No Room at the Inn: the causes of gridlock – leaving the old in limbo*. London, Liberal Democrats.
- Care Development Group (2001) *Fair Care for Older People*. Edinburgh, TSO.
- Carers National Association (1997) *Still Battling? The Carers Act One Year On*. London, Carers National Association.
- Clark H, Dyer H and Hartman L (1996) *Going Home: older people leaving hospital*. Bristol, Policy Press.
- Clode D (2002) Another fine mess. *Community Care*, 11–17 July, 30–32.
- Coast J, Inglis A, Morgan K, Gray S, Kammerling M and Frankel S (1995) The hospital admissions study in England: are there alternatives to emergency hospital admission? *Journal of Epidemiology and Community Health* **49**: 194–199.
- Coast J, Inglis A and Frankel S (1996a) Alternatives to hospital care: what are they and who should decide? *British Medical Journal* **312**: 162–166.
- Coast J, Peters T and Inglis A (1996b) Factors associated with inappropriate emergency hospital admission in the UK. *International Journal for Quality in Health Care* **8**: 31–39.
- Coid J and Crome P (1986) Bed blocking in Bromley. *British Medical Journal* **292**: 1253–1256.
- Community Care (1998) Councils spell out cost of cuts. *Community Care*, 2–8 July, 2.
- Community Care (2000) Milburn moots. *Community Care*, 15–21 June, 17.
- Connelly MA and Ritchie S (1997) An audit of in-patients aged 18–65 in acute psychiatric wards who are inappropriately placed three months after admission. *Health Bulletin* **55**: 156–161.
- Cormie J (1999) The Fife User Panels Project: empowering older people. In: M Barnes and L Warren (eds) *Paths to Empowerment*. Bristol, Policy Press.
- Cumella S, Marston G and Roy A (1998) Bed blockage in an acute admission service for people with a learning difficulty. *British Journal of Learning Disabilities* **26**: 118–121.
- Davies M (1979) Swapping the old around. *Community Care*, 18 October, 16–17.
- Department of Health (1989a) *Caring for People: community care in the next decade and beyond*. London, HMSO.
- Department of Health (1989b) *Discharge of Patients from Hospital*. HC(89)5, LAC(89)7 (includes accompanying booklet).

- Department of Health (1990) *Community Care in the Next Decade and Beyond: policy guidance*. London, HMSO.
- Department of Health (1991) *The Patient's Charter: raising the standard*. London, HMSO.
- Department of Health (1992a) *Implementing Caring for People*. EL(92)13, CI(92)10.
- Department of Health (1992b) *Implementing Caring for People*. EL(92)65, CI(92)30.
- Department of Health (1992c) *Community Care*. LASSL(92)8.
- Department of Health (1992d) *Department of Health Memorandum on the Financing of Community Care Arrangements after April 1993 and on Individual Choice of Residential Accommodation*. London, Department of Health.
- Department of Health (1995) *NHS Responsibilities for Meeting Continuing Health Care Needs*. HSG(95)8, LAC(95)5.
- Department of Health (1996) *Carers (Recognition and Services) Act 1995: policy guidance*. London, Department of Health.
- Department of Health (1997a) *Managing Winter 1997/98*. MISC(97)62.
- Department of Health (1997b) *NHS Finance – Additional Money for Patient Care*. EL(97)61.
- Department of Health (1997c) *Better Services for Vulnerable People*. EL(97)62, CI(97)24.
- Department of Health (1997d) *The New NHS: modern, dependable*. London, TSO.
- Department of Health (1998a) *Partnership in Action: new opportunities for joint working between health and social services – a discussion document*. London, Department of Health.
- Department of Health (1998b) *Modernising Social Services: promoting independence, improving protection, raising standards*. London, TSO.
- Department of Health (1998c) *Modernising Health and Social Services: national priorities guidance, 1999/00–2001/02*. London, Department of Health.
- Department of Health (1998d) *Additional Money for Patient Care this Winter*. HSC 1998/209.
- Department of Health (1999a) *Ex parte Coughlan: follow up action*. HSC 1999/180, LAC(99)30.
- Department of Health (1999b) *The Health Act 1999*. London, TSO.
- Department of Health (1999c) *The Relationship between Health and Social Services: government response to the first report of the Health Committee on the relationship between health and social services – session 1998–99*. London, TSO.
- Department of Health (2000a) *The NHS Plan: a plan for investment, a plan for reform*. London, Department of Health.
- Department of Health (2000b) *Shaping the Future NHS: long term planning for hospitals and related services – consultation document on the findings of the National Beds Inquiry*. London, Department of Health.
- Department of Health (2000c) *Promoting Independence: partnership, prevention and carers grants – conditions and allocations 2000/2001*. LAC(2000)6.
- Department of Health (2000d) *Caring about Carers: a national strategy for carers* (2e). London, Department of Health.
- Department of Health (2000e) *The NHS Plan Implementation Programme*. London, Department of Health.

- Department of Health (2000f) *Winter 2000/01: capacity planning for health and social care*. HSC 2000/016, LAC(2000)14.
- Department of Health (2001a) *Guide to Integrating Community Equipment Stores*. London, Department of Health.
- Department of Health (2001b) *Care Trusts: emerging framework*. London, Department of Health.
- Department of Health (2001c) *The Health and Social Care Act 2001*. London, TSO.
- Department of Health (2001d) *The Single Assessment Process: consultation papers and progress*. Available online via www.doh.gov.uk/scg/sap/index.htm (accessed 20/08/01).
- Department of Health (2001e) *Intermediate Care*. HSC 2001/001, LAC(2001)1.
- Department of Health (2001f) *Shifting the Balance of Power within the NHS: securing delivery*. London, Department of Health.
- Department of Health (2001g) *Continuing Care: NHS and local councils' responsibilities*. HSC 2001/015, LAC(2001)18.
- Department of Health (2001h) *£300 Million 'Cash for Change' Initiative to Tackle 'Bed-blocking'*. Press release 2001/0464. London, Department of Health.
- Department of Health (2001i) *Building Capacity and Partnership in Care: an agreement between the statutory and the independent social care, health care and housing sectors*. London, Department of Health.
- Department of Health (2001j) *Promoting Independence Grant 2001–02*. Available online via www.doh.gov.uk/scg/independencegrant/index.htm (accessed 16/07/01).
- Department of Health (2001k) *Carers and Disabled Children Act 2000: carers and people with parental responsibilities for disabled children – policy guidance and practice guidance*. London, Department of Health.
- Department of Health (2001l) *2001/2002: arrangements for whole system capacity planning – emergency, elective and social care*. HSC 2001/014, LAC(2001)17.
- Department of Health (2001m) *National Service Framework for Older People: modern standards and service models*. London, Department of Health.
- Department of Health (2001n) *Care Homes for Older People: national minimum standards*. London, TSO.
- Department of Health (2001o) *A Guide to Contracting for Intermediate Care Services*. Available online via www.doh.gov.uk/intermediatecare/index.htm (accessed 14/09/01).
- Department of Health (2001p) *New Award Scheme gets Royal Seal of Approval*. Press release 2001/0367. London, Department of Health.
- Department of Health (2001q) *Intermediate Care – £66 Million Capital Investment Bids and Criteria*. 2 November.
- Department of Health (2002a) *Health and Social Care Change Agent Team*. Available online via www.doh.gov.uk/jointunit/changeagentsintro.htm (accessed 24/07/2002).
- Department of Health (2002b) *Delivering the NHS Plan: next steps on investment, next steps on reform*. London, Department of Health.

- Department of Health (2002c) *Full Text of Alan Milburn's Statement on Services for Older People*. Available online via www.society.guardian.co.uk/longtermcare/story/0,8150,7620928,00.html (accessed 24/07/2002).
- Department of Health (2002d) *Implementing Reimbursement around Discharge from Hospital* (consultation document). London, Department of Health.
- Department of Health (2002e) *Government Response to the Health Select Committee Third Report of Session 2001–02 on Delayed Discharges*. London, Department of Health.
- Department of Health (n.d.) *Shaping the Future NHS: long term planning for hospitals and related services – response to the consultation exercise on the findings of the National Beds Inquiry*. London, Department of Health.
- Department of Health/Office for National Statistics (2001) *Social Services Performance Assessment Framework Indicators, 2000–2001*. London, Government Statistical Service/Department of Health.
- Department of Health/Social Services Inspectorate (SSI) (1992a) *Social Services for Hospital Patients I: working at the interface*. London, Department of Health.
- Department of Health/SSI (1992b) *Social Services for Hospital Patients II: the implications for community care*. London, Department of Health.
- Department of Health/SSI (1993) *Social Services for Hospital Patients III: users and carers perspective*. London, Department of Health.
- Department of Health/SSI (1995) *Moving On: report of the national inspection of social services department arrangements for the discharge of older people from hospital to residential or nursing home care*. London, Department of Health.
- Department of Health/SSI (2001) *Improving Older People's Services: inspection of social care services for older people*. London, Department of Health.
- Department of Health/SSI/Scottish Office Social Work Services Group (SWSG) (1991) *Care Management and Assessment: managers' guide*. London, HMSO.
- Department of Health, Social Services and Public Safety (DHSSPS)/SSI (1997) *From Hospital to Home: a multi-disciplinary inspection of trust arrangements for the discharge of older people from hospital to their own home, residential or nursing home care*. Belfast, TSO Northern Ireland.
- DHSSPS/SSI (2000) *An Introduction to Personal Social Services*. Belfast, SSI.
- Dickinson MJ and Singh I (1991) Mental handicap and the new long stay. *Psychiatric Bulletin* **15**: 334–335.
- Dymond D (1998) Why this photo reveals the truth about our slum NHS. *Daily Mail*, 30 December.
- ESAT (1998) *Second Report from the Emergency Services Action Team (ESAT)*. London, Department of Health.
- Festing S (1999) *The Dignity on the Ward Manual (Background Information): the care of older people in NHS hospital trusts*. London, Help the Aged.
- Fife Council Home Care Service (n.d.) *Pilot Hospital Discharge Project: evaluation report*. Fife, Fife Council Home Care Service (Central).
- Fife User Panels Project (1994) *Health Care Issues: comments made by panel members from March 1993–1994*. Fife, Fife User Panels Project.

- Fulop N, Koffman J and Hudson M (1992) Challenging bed behaviours: the use of acute psychiatric beds in an inner-London District Health Authority. *Journal of Mental Health* **1**: 335–341.
- Fulop NJ, Koffman J, Carson S, Robinson A, Pashley D and Coleman K (1996) Use of psychiatric beds: a point prevalence study in North and South Thames regions. *Journal of Public Health Medicine* **18**: 207–216.
- Gertman PM and Restuccia JD (1981) The Appropriateness Evaluation Protocol: a technique for assessing unnecessary days of hospital care. *Medical Care* **8**: 855–871.
- Glasby J (1999) *Poverty and Opportunity: one hundred years of the Birmingham Settlement*. Studley, Brewin Books.
- Glasby J (ed.) (2000a) *'Back to the Future' – the History of the Settlement Movement and its Relevance for Organisations Today*. Birmingham, Department of Social Policy and Social Work, University of Birmingham.
- Glasby J (2000b) Taking the stress out of social work: a multidimensional model of occupational stress. *Practice* **12**: 29–44.
- Glasby J (2000c) The NHS Plan: maintaining the human touch. *Managing Community Care* **8**: 11–14.
- Glasby J (2001a) *The Politics of Poverty: Settlements and social work practice*. (Unpublished paper presented at Toynbee Hall, London, 22 September 2001.)
- Glasby J (2001b) On shaky foundations. *Community Care*, 2–8 August, 30.
- Glasby J (2001c) Who cares wins. *Nursing Older People* **13**: 6.
- Glasby J (2002a) A drop in the ocean? *Nursing Older People* **13**: 6.
- Glasby J (2002b) Planning and preparing for intermediate care services. In: S Wade (ed.) *Intermediate Care and Older People: Cinderella or Rolls Royce service*. London, Whurr Publishers.
- Glasby J (2002c) *Surviving Change: a case study of the Birmingham Settlement (1899–1999)* (PhD thesis). Department of Social Policy and Social Work, University of Birmingham.
- Glasby J (2002d) Charging ahead. *Nursing Older People* **13**: 7.
- Glasby J (2002e) Making social services pay is wrong … *Health Service Journal* **112**: 24.
- Glasby J (forthcoming) Bringing down the 'Berlin Wall': the health and social care divide. *British Journal of Social Work.*
- Glasby J and Glasby J (1999) *Paying for Social Services: social services and local government finance*. Birmingham, PEPAR Publications.
- Glasby J and Glasby J (2002) *Cash for Caring: a practical guide to social services finance*. Lyme Regis, Russell House.
- Glasby J, Lester H, Briscoe J, Clark M, Rose S and England L (2003) *Cases for Change in Mental Health*. London, Department of Health/National Institute for Mental Health.
- Glasby J and Littlechild R (2000a) *The Health and Social Care Divide: the experiences of older people*. Birmingham, PEPAR Publications.
- Glasby J and Littlechild R (2000b) Fighting fires? – emergency hospital admission and the concept of prevention. *Journal of Management in Medicine* **14**: 109–118.

- Glasby J and Littlechild R (2000c) Falling into the chasm. *Nursing Older People* **12**: 32–33.
- Glasby J and Littlechild R (2001) Inappropriate admissions: patient participation in research. *British Journal of Nursing* **10**: 738–741.
- Glasby J and Littlechild R (2002) *Social Work and Direct Payments*. Bristol, Policy Press.
- Glendinning C (2002) A charge too far. *Community Care*, 11–17 July, 34–36.
- Godfrey M and Moore J (1996) *Hospital Discharge: user, carer and professional perspectives*. Leeds, Nuffield Institute for Health Community Care Division.
- Goodwin N (2002) Intermediate care for older people: policy, practice and evaluation. *HSMC Newsletter* **8**: 9.
- Griffiths R (1988) *Community Care: agenda for action – a report to the Secretary of State for Social Services by Sir Roy Griffiths*. London, HMSO.
- Hardy B, Hudson B and Waddington E (2000) *What Makes a Good Partnership? A Partnership Assessment Tool*. Leeds, Nuffield Institute for Health Community Care Division.
- Hare P and Newbronner L (2001) *Hospital Discharges and Disability: a survey of the views and experiences of disabled people and carers in the East Riding of Yorkshire*. York, Acton.Shapiro.
- Heartlands Hospital Trust/Birmingham Social Services Department (n.d.) *Appropriate Bed Occupancy Pilot*. Unpublished report, Heartlands Hospital/Birmingham Social Services Department.
- Help the Aged (2001) *Help the Aged Intermediate Care Programme for Older People: older people's experiences of intermediate care – a research brief*. London, Help the Aged.
- Henwood M (ed.) (1994) *Hospital Discharge Workbook: a manual on hospital discharge practice*. London, Department of Health.
- Henwood M (1998) *Ignored and Invisible: carers' experience of the NHS*. London, Carers National Association.
- Henwood M and Wistow G (1993) *Hospital Discharge and Community Care: early days*. Leeds, Nuffield Institute for Health.
- Henwood M, Hardy B, Hudson B and Wistow G (1997) *Inter-agency Collaboration: hospital discharge and continuing care sub-study*. Leeds, Nuffield Institute for Health Community Care Division.
- Hill M and Macgregor G (2001) *Health's Forgotten Partners? How Carers are Supported through Hospital Discharge*. London, Carers UK.
- Holzhausen E (2001) *'You Can Take Him Home Now.' Carers' Experiences of Hospital Discharge*. London, Carers National Association.
- HOPe (2000) *Our Future Health: older people's priorities for health and social care*. London, Help the Aged.
- Horne D (1998) *Getting Better? Inspection of Hospital Discharge (Care Management) Arrangements for Older People*. London, Department of Health.
- House of Commons Debates (1997) *Hansard*, 9 December, col 802.
- House of Commons Health Committee (1999) *The Relationship between Health and Social Services* (first report). London, TSO.

- House of Commons Health Committee (2002) *Delayed Discharges* (third report). London, TSO.
- House of Commons Select Committee on Public Accounts (2001) *Inpatient Admission, Bed Management and Patient Discharge in NHS Acute Hospitals*. Available online via www.publications.parliament.uk/pa/cm200001cmselect/cmpubacc/135/13502.htm (accessed 25/01/02).
- Huber N (2000) Social services fear commissioning takeover by primary care trusts. *Community Care*, 15–21 June, 2–3.
- Hudson B (2000) Adult Care. In: M Hill (ed.) *Local Authority Social Services: an introduction*. London, Blackwell.
- Hudson B, Hardy B, Henwood M and Wistow G (1997) *Inter-agency Collaboration: final report*. Leeds, Nuffield Institute for Health Community Care Division.
- Hudson B, Young R, Hardy B and Glendinning C (2001) *National Evaluation of Notifications for Use of the Section 31 Partnership Flexibilities of the Health Act 1999: interim report*. Leeds/Manchester, Nuffield Institute for Health/National Primary Care Research and Development Centre.
- Huws Jones R (1952) Old people's welfare – successes and failures. *Social Service Quarterly* **26**: 19–22.
- ISD Scotland (2000) *Patients Ready for Discharge in the NHS in Scotland: figures from 30 September 2000 census*. Available online via www.show.scot.nhs.uk/isd/publications/pubsp-r.htm (accessed 29/11/01).
- ISD Scotland (2001a) *Patients Ready for Discharge in NHS Scotland: figures from 15 January 2001 census*. Available online via www.show.scot.nhs.uk/isd/publications/pubsp-r.htm (accessed 29/11/01).
- ISD Scotland (2001b) *Patients Ready for Discharge in NHS Scotland: figures from 15 April 2001 census*. Available online via www.show.scot.nhs.uk/isd/publications/pubsp-r.htm (accessed 29/11/01).
- ISD Scotland (2001c) *Patients Ready for Discharge in NHS Scotland: figures from 15 July 2001 census*. Available online via www.show.scot.nhs.uk/isd/publications/pubsp-r.htm (accessed 29/11/01).
- ISD Scotland (2002) *Patients Ready for Discharge in NHS Scotland: figures from 15 October 2001 census*. Available online via www.show.scot.nhs.uk/isd/publications/pubsp-r.htm (accessed 29/11/01).
- Jones D and Lester C (1995) Patients' opinions of hospital care and discharge. In: G Wilson (ed.) *Community Care: asking the users*. London, Chapman & Hall.
- Khan A, Cumella S, Krishnan V, Iqbal M, Corbett J and Clarke D (1993) New long-stay patients at a mental handicap hospital. *Mental Handicap Research* **6**: 165–173.
- Koffman J, Fulop N, Pashley D and Coleman K (1996) No way out: the delayed discharge of elderly mentally ill acute and assessment patients in North and South Thames regions. *Age and Ageing* **25**: 268–272.
- Laing W (1993) *Financing Long-term Care: the crucial debate*. London, Age Concern England.

- Lelliott P, Wing J and Clifford P (1994) A national audit of new long-stay psychiatric patients II: impact on services. *British Journal of Psychiatry* **165**: 170–178.
- Lewis J (1995) *The Voluntary Sector, the State and Social Work in Britain: the Charity Organisation Society/Family Welfare Association since 1868.* Aldershot, Edward Elgar.
- Lewis J (2001) Older people and the health–social care boundary in the UK: half a century of hidden policy conflict. *Social Policy and Administration* **35**: 343–359.
- Liberal Democrats (2002a) *88,000 Operations a Year Unable to Take Place due to 1,400 Years of Bed Blocking.* London, Liberal Democrats press release, 15/01/02.
- Liberal Democrats (2002b) *Delayed Discharge Costs NHS £23 Million.* London, Liberal Democrats press release, 21/01/02.
- Liberal Democrats (2002c) *Bed Blocking Problems get Worse as 2 in 5 Patients are Stuck in Hospital for a Month or More.* London, Liberal Democrats press release, 27/01/02.
- Littlechild R and Glasby J (2000) Older people as 'participating patients'. In: H Kemshall and R Littlechild (eds) *User Involvement and Participation in Social Care.* London, Jessica Kingsley.
- Littlechild R and Glasby J (2001) Emergency hospital admissions: older patients' perceptions. *Education and Ageing* **16**: 77–89.
- Littlechild R, Smallwood H, Jeffes L and Chesterman M (1995) Care management for older people discharged from hospital. *Elders* **4**: 37–50.
- Macmillan MS, Tierney AJ, Atkinson FI, King C and Worth A (1993) *A National Survey of General Practitioners' Experience and Views relating to Discharge of Elderly People following Acute Hospital Care* (3rd Supplementary Report to the Report on 'Discharge of Patients from Hospital'). Nursing Research Unit, Department of Nursing Studies, University of Edinburgh.
- Maddison A (1954) Mental sickness provision. *Hospital and Social Service Journal*, 26 September, 983.
- Maloney M (2001) Opponents air health worries. *Shuttle Times and News*, 18 January, 4.
- Mandelstam M (1999) *Community Care Practice and the Law* (2e). London, Jessica Kingsley.
- Marks L (1994) *Seamless Care or Patchwork Quilt? Discharging Patients from Acute Hospital Care* (research report 17). London, King's Fund Institute.
- Marsh P (2001a) Hit squad fears for hospitals: government may step in. *Birmingham Evening Mail*, 28 June, 4.
- Marsh P (2001b) MS mum 'left to rot in hospital'. *Birmingham Evening Mail*, 20 November, 15.
- Marsh P (2001c) City pays price for beds crisis. *Birmingham Evening Mail*, 2 July, 1.
- McCulloch P, Bowyer J, Fitzsimmons T, Johnson M, Lowe D and Ward R (1997) Emergency admission of patients to general surgical beds: attitudes of general practitioners, surgical trainees, and consultants in Liverpool, UK. *Journal of Epidemiology and Community Health* **51**: 315–319.
- McDonagh MS, Smith DH and Goddard M (2000) Measuring appropriate use of acute beds: a systematic review of methods and results. *Health Policy* **53**: 157–184.

- Means R (1986) The development of social services: historical perspectives. In: C Phillipson and A Walker (eds) *Ageing and Social Policy: a critical assessment*. Aldershot, Gower.
- Means R and Smith R (1998a) *Community Care: policy and practice* (2e). Basingstoke, Macmillan.
- Means R and Smith R (1998b) *From Poor Law to Community Care: the development of welfare services for elderly people, 1939–1971* (2e). Bristol, Policy Press.
- Means R, Brenton M, Harrison L and Heywood F (1997) *Making Partnerships Work in Community Care: a guide for practitioners in housing, health and social services*. Bristol, Policy Press.
- Millar B (1998) Honourable discharge. *Health Service Journal*, 8 January, 26–29.
- Millennium Executive Team (2000) *Millennium Executive Team Report on Winter 1999/2000*. London, Department of Health.
- Minghella E and Ford R (1997) Focal points? *Health Service Journal* **107**: 36–37.
- Ministry of Health (1957a) *Local Authority Services for the Chronic Sick and Infirm*. 14/57.
- Ministry of Health (1957b) *Geriatric Services and the Care of the Chronic Sick*. HM(57) 86.
- Ministry of Health (1963) *Discharge of Patients from Hospital and Arrangements for After-Care*. HM(63) 24.
- Ministry of Health (1965) *The Care of the Elderly in Hospitals and Residential Homes*. 18/65.
- Moore A (2002) Canterbury tales. *Health Service Journal*, 17 January, 12–13.
- Moore C (1998) Discharge from an acute psychiatric ward. *Nursing Times* **94**: 56–59.
- Moore W (1995) *Emergency Admissions: the management challenge*. Birmingham, NAHAT.
- Murphy FW (1977) Blocked beds. *British Medical Journal* i: 1395–1396.
- Namdaran F, Burnet C and Munroe S (1992) Bed blocking in Edinburgh hospitals. *Health Bulletin* **50**: 223–227.
- National Assembly for Wales (2000) *Delayed Transfers of Care Definitions*. Cardiff, National Assembly for Wales.
- National Audit Office (2000) *Inpatient Admissions and Bed Management in NHS Acute Hospitals*. London, TSO.
- Neill J and Williams J (1992) *Leaving Hospital: older people and their discharge to community care*. London, HMSO.
- Netten A, Rees T and Harrison G (2001) *Unit Costs of Health and Social Care 2001*. Available online via www.ukc.ac.uk/PSSRU (accessed 25/01/02).
- NHS Confederation (1997) *Tackling Emergency Admissions: policy into practice*. Birmingham, NHS Confederation.
- NHS Executive (2000) *Quality and Performance in the NHS: NHS performance indicators*. London, Department of Health.
- Owen V (1998) Queue here for misery. *Daily Mail*, 29 December.
- Phillipson J and Williams J (1995) *Action on Hospital Discharge*. London, NISW.

- Reed J and Morgan D (1999) Discharging older people from hospital to care homes: implications for nursing. *Journal of Advanced Nursing* **29**: 819–825.
- Rickford F (2001) Can things only get better? *Community Care*, 26 July, 18–19.
- Roberts P and Houghton M (1996) In search of a block buster. *Health Service Journal*, 5 December, 28–29.
- Royal Commission on Long Term Care (1999) *With Respect to Old Age: long term care – rights and responsibilities*. London, TSO.
- Rubin SG and Davies GH (1975) Bed blocking by elderly patients in general hospital wards. *Age and Ageing* **4**: 142–147.
- Sainsbury Centre for Mental Health (1998) *Acute Problems: a survey of the quality of care in acute psychiatric wards*. London, Sainsbury Centre.
- Samson E (1944) *Old Age in the New World*. London, Pilot Press.
- Scottish Executive (2000) *Delayed Discharge Learning Network*. Unpublished report, Scottish Executive Delayed Discharge Learning Network.
- Shepherd G, Beardsmoore A, Moore C, Hardy P and Muijen M (1997) Relation between bed use, social deprivation, and overall bed availability in acute adult psychiatric units, and alternative residential options: a cross sectional survey, one day census data, and staff interviews. *British Medical Journal* **314**: 262–266.
- Social Policy Ageing Information Network (SPAIN) (2001) *The Underfunding of Social Care and its Consequences for Older People*. Available online via www.helptheaged. org.uk (accessed 08/02/02).
- Strumwasser I, Paranjpe N, Ronis D, Share D and Sell L (1990) Reliability and validity of utilization review criteria. *Medical Care* **28**: 95–111.
- Taraborrelli P, Wood F, Bloor M, Pithouse A and Parry O (1998) *Hospital Discharge for Frail Older People: a literature review with practice case studies*. Edinburgh, Scottish Office Central Research Unit.
- Thane P (1996) *Foundations of the Welfare State* (2e). London, Routledge.
- Thomas R (2001) UK economic policy: the Conservative legacy and New Labour's third way. In: S Savage and R Atkinson (eds) *Public Policy under Blair*. Basingstoke, Palgrave.
- Thompson N (2001) *Anti-discriminatory Practice* (3e). Basingstoke, Palgrave.
- Thorne A (2001) Blood-letting politics over Health Concern. *Birmingham Post*, 2 February.
- Tierney AJ, Closs SJ, Hunter HC and Macmillan MS (1993a) Experiences of elderly patients concerning discharge from hospital. *Journal of Clinical Nursing* **2**: 179–185.
- Tierney AJ, Closs SJ, King C, Worth A and Macmillan MS (1993b) *A National Survey of Current Discharge Planning Practice in Acute Hospital Wards throughout Scotland* (1st Supplementary Report to the Report on 'Discharge of Patients from Hospital'). Nursing Research Unit, Department of Nursing Studies, University of Edinburgh.
- Tierney AJ, Macmillan MS, Worth A and King C (1994a) Discharge of patients from hospital – current practice and perceptions of hospital and community staff in Scotland. *Health Bulletin* **52**: 479–491.

- Tierney A, Worth A, Closs SJ, King C and Macmillan M (1994b) Older patients' experiences of discharge from hospital. *Nursing Times* **25**: 36–39.
- Timmins N (2001) Anger over local hospital gives real bite to underdog doctor's campaign. *Financial Times*, 28 May.
- Tinker A (1997) *Older People in Modern Society* (4e). London, Longman.
- Vaughan B and Lathlean J (1999) *Intermediate Care: models in practice*. London, King's Fund.
- Victor C (1991) *Health and Health Care in Later Life*. Milton Keynes, Open University Press.
- Victor C (1997) *Community Care and Older People*. Cheltenham, Stanley Thomas.
- Victor C, Nazareth B, Hudson M and Fulop N (1993a) The inappropriate use of acute hospital beds in an inner London District Health Authority. *Health Trends* **25**: 94–97.
- Victor C, Young E, Hudson M and Wallace P (1993b) Whose responsibility is it anyway? Hospital admission and discharge of older people in an inner-London District Health Authority. *Journal of Advanced Nursing* **18**: 1297–1304.
- Victor C, Healy J, Thomas A and Sargeant J (2000) Older patients and delayed discharge from hospital. *Health and Social Care in the Community* **8**: 443–452.
- Warren M (1951) The elderly in the community. *Social Service Quarterly* **24**: 102–106.
- White C (1999) Health emergency. *Community Care*, 28 January – 3 February, 18–19.
- Winchester P (2000) Care sector hopes to bury NHS merger proposal. *Community Care*, 29 June – 5 July, 10–11.
- Wistow G (1996) The changing scene in Britain. In: T Harding, B Meredith and G Wistow (eds) *Options for Long Term Care: economic, social and ethical choices*. London, HMSO.
- Worth A, Tierney AJ, Macmillan MS, King C and Atkinson FI (1993) *A National Survey of Community Nursing Staff's Experience and Views Relating to Discharge of Elderly People following Acute Hospital Care* (2nd Supplementary Report to the Report on 'Discharge of Patients from Hospital'). Nursing Research Unit, Department of Nursing Studies, University of Edinburgh.

Further reading

- Age Concern (1997) *Hospital Discharge Arrangements and NHS Continuing Health Care Services* (Fact Sheet 37). London, Age Concern England.
- Age Concern (2000) *Hospital Discharge Arrangements and NHS Continuing Health Care Services*. Available online via www.ageconcern.org.uk (accessed 30/08/01).
- Ahulu S (1995) Discharge to the community of older patients from hospital. *Nursing Times* **91**: 29–30.
- Allen I, Dalley G and Leat D (1992) *Monitoring Change in Social Services Departments*. London, Policy Studies Institute for the Association of Directors of Social Services.
- Alridge J (1999) Trauma as wards go on red alert. *The Observer*, 10 January.
- Arskey H, Heaton J and Sloper P (1998) Tell it like it is. *Health Service Journal*, 22 January, 32–33.
- Baldwin S and Lunt N (1996) *Charging Ahead: the development of local authority charging policies for community care*. Bristol, Policy Press in association with Joseph Rowntree Foundation and Community Care.
- Barnes D (1997) *Older People with Mental Health Problems Living Alone: anybody's priority?* London, Department of Health.
- Barrett G and Hudson M (1997) Changes in district nursing workload. *Journal of Community Nursing* **11**: 4–8.
- Beattie A and Brodie J (1996) *Perspectives on Hospital Aftercare*. London, Age Concern London.
- Bebbington A and Charnley H (1990) Community care for the elderly: rhetoric and reality. *British Journal of Social Work* **20**: 409–432.
- Beech R, Challah S and Ingram R (1987) Impact of cuts in acute beds on services for patients. *British Medical Journal* **294**: 685–688.
- BGS/ADSS/RCN (1995) *The Discharge of Elderly Persons from Hospital for Community Care*. Wolverhampton, BGS/ADSS/RCN.
- Bowl R (1986) Social work with old people. In: C Phillipson and A Walker (eds) *Ageing and Social Policy: a critical assessment*. Aldershot, Gower.
- Bridges J, Meyer J, Davidson D, Harris J and Glynn M (1999) Smooth passage. *Health Service Journal*, 17 June, 24–25.
- Brown C (1997) Doctors reveal winter chaos in NHS. *The Independent*, 10 January.
- Carvel J (2001) City's hospitals jammed by care crisis. *The Guardian*, 11 June, 8.
- Clarke L (1984) *Domiciliary Services for the Elderly*. London, Croom Helm.
- Community Care (1998) Director admits cash shortage blocked beds. *Community Care*, 2–8 July, 4.
- Cotter A, Meyer J and Roberts S (1998) The transition from hospital to long-term institutional care. *Nursing Times* **94**: 54–56.
- Cowley P (1998) Independence day. *Nursing Times* **94**: 36–37.
- Department of Health (1989) *Working for Patients*. London, HMSO.

- Department of Health (1995) *Discharge from NHS Inpatient Care of People with Continuing Health or Social Care Needs: arrangements for reviewing decisions on eligibility for NHS inpatient care.* HSG(95)39, LAC(95)17.
- Department of Health (1995) *Developing Continuing Health Care Policies: a checklist for purchasers.*
- Department of Health (1995) *Developing and Implementing Eligibility Criteria for Continuing Health Care: a checklist for purchasers.*
- Department of Health (1995) *NHS Responsibilities for Meeting Continuing Health Care Needs – NHS Executive/SSI monitoring.* EL(95)88, CI(95)37.
- Department of Health (1996) *NHS Responsibilities for Meeting Continuing Health Care Needs – Current Progress and Future Priorities.* EL(96)8, CI(96)5.
- Department of Health (1996) *Progress in Practice: initial evaluation of the impact of the continuing care guidance.* EL(96)89, CI(96)35.
- Department of Health (1996) *Funding for Priority Services 1996/97 and 1997/98.* EL(96)109.
- Department of Health (1997) *Community Care – Special Transitional Grant Conditions and Indicative Allocations 1998/99.* LASSL(97)25.
- Department of Health (1997) *Our Healthier Nation: a contract for health.* London, TSO.
- Department of Health (1999) *Saving Lives: our healthier nation.* London, TSO.
- Department of Health (1999) *Statement on Coughlan Judgement.* Department of Health press release, 16 July.
- Department of Health (2001) *Shifting the Balance of Power: securing delivery – human resources framework.* London, Department of Health.
- Department of Health/SSI (1995) *Caring for People at Home: an overview of the national inspection of social services department arrangements for the assessment and delivery of home care services.* London, Department of Health.
- Department of Health/SSI (1996) *Caring for People at Home – part II: report of a second inspection of arrangements for assessment and delivery of home care services.* London, Department of Health.
- Department of Health/SSI (1997) *At Home with Dementia: inspection of services for older people with dementia in the community.* London, Department of Health.
- Department of Health/SSI/Scottish Office Social Work Services Group (SWSG) (1991) *Care Management and Assessment: practitioners' guide.* London, HMSO.
- Department of Health/SSI/SWSG (1991) *Care Management and Assessment: summary of practice guidance.* London, HMSO.
- Dyer C (1998) Judge rules NHS cannot jettison long-term care. *The Guardian*, 12 December.
- George M (1996) Pass the patient. *Community Care*, 14 March, 20–21.
- Glasby J (1999) The art of conversation. *Journal of Practice and Development* 7: 20–26.
- Glasby J (2000) Mixed blessings: is the NHS Plan revolutionary? *British Journal of Nursing* 9: 2001.

- Godlove C and Mann A (1980) Thirty years of the welfare state: current issues in British social policy for the aged. *Aged Care and Services Review* **2**: 1–12.
- Godwin N and Shapiro J (2001) *The Road to Integrated Care Working* (Research report number 39). Birmingham, Health Services Management Centre.
- Hall D and Bytheway B (1982) The blocked bed: definition of a problem. *Social Science and Medicine* **16**: 1985–1991.
- Harrison S (1988) Changing admission patterns of short-stay geriatric patients. *Nursing Times* **84**: 53–55.
- Heaton J, Arskey H and Sloper P (1999) Carers' experiences of hospital discharge and continuing care in the community. *Health and Social Care in the Community* **7**: 91–99.
- Help the Aged (1995) *Coming Out of Hospital* (revised 2001). London, Help the Aged.
- Henwood M (1990) *Community Care and Older People: policy, practice and research review*. London, Family Policy Studies Centre.
- Henwood M (1992) Twilight zone. *Health Service Journal*, 5 November, 28–30.
- Henwood M (1995) Strained relations. *Health Service Journal*, 6 July, 22–23.
- Henwood M (1996) Silent progress. *Health Service Journal*, 21 November, 24–25.
- Henwood M (1997) Discharge account. *Community Care*, 6–12 November, 28–29.
- House of Commons Social Services Committee (1985) *Second Report: community care.* (House of Commons Paper 13–1, Session 1984–1985). London, HMSO.
- Hunter M (1999) Pressure mounts on government to clarify arrangements for long-term nursing care. *Community Care*, 22–28 July, 4–5.
- Keys R (1997) Right approach. *Health Service Journal*, 25 September, 28–29.
- Mackintosh J, McKeown T and Garratt F (1961) An examination of the need for hospital admission. *Lancet* **1**: 815–818.
- Marshall M (1990) Proud to be old. In: E McEwen (ed.) *Age: the unrecognised discrimination*. London, Age Concern England.
- McLean CA (1988) Essex hospital discharge survey. *Social Services Research* **2**: 13–17.
- National Assembly for Wales (2001) *Delayed transfers of care: guidance notes for health authorities, trusts and local authorities.* Cardiff, National Assembly for Wales.
- Nixon A, Whitter M and Stitt P (1998) Audit in practice: planning for discharge from hospital. *Nursing Standard* **12**: 35–38.
- Nocon A and Baldwin S (1998) *Trends in Rehabilitation Policy: a review of the literature.* London, King's Fund.
- Pattie A and Heaton J (1990) *A Comparative Study of Dependency and Provision of Care for the Elderly in the State and Private Sectors in York Health District.* York, Yorkshire Regional Health Authority.
- Powell J, Lovelock R, Bray J and Philp I (1994) Quality issues in discharge from hospital – the views of older people and their carers. *Social Services Research* **1**: 42–55.
- Rayner H (1998) Taking a day off. *Health Service Journal*, 8 January, 32–33.

- Reed J and Stanley D (2000) Discharge from hospital to care homes: professional boundaries and interfaces. In: AM Warnes, L Warren and M Nolan (eds) *Care Services in Later Life: transformations and critiques*. London, Jessica Kingsley.
- Reid J, Dexter E, Payne M and Brooks R (1998) *Appropriateness of Acute Medical Admissions in the Elderly*. Unpublished poster presentation at the British Geriatrics Society conference, Edinburgh, March 1998.
- Sansom D and Cumella S (1995) One hundred admissions to a regional secure unit for people with a learning disability. *Journal of Forensic Psychiatry* **6**: 267–276.
- Scottish Office (1993) *Discharge From Hospitals: a guide to good practice*. Edinburgh, Management Executive of the National Health Service in Scotland.
- Seymour D and Pringle R (1983) Surgical emergencies in the elderly: can they be prevented? *Health Bulletin* **41**: 112–131.
- Shaw T (1998) Paralysed resident of home wins care case. *The Telegraph*, 12 December.
- Shore P (1998) Ready, steady, go. *Health Service Journal*, 8 January, 30–31.
- Sidell M (1995) *Health in Old Age: myth, mystery and management*. Buckingham, Open University Press.
- Sinclair A and Dickinson E (1998) *Effective Practice in Rehabilitation: evidence from systematic reviews*. London, King's Fund.
- Sinclair I and Williams J (1990) Domiciliary services. In: I Sinclair, R Parker, D Leat and J Williams (eds) *The Kaleidoscope of Care: a review of research on welfare provision for elderly people*. London, HMSO.
- Sinclair I, Parker R, Leat D and Williams J (1990) *The Kaleidoscope of Care: a review of research on welfare provision for elderly people*. London, HMSO.
- Smallwood H and Jeffes L (n.d.) *Hereford Hospital Discharge Project*. Unpublished report, Hereford and Worcester County Council Social Services Department.
- Smith H, Pryce A, Carlisle L, Jones J, Scarpello J and Pantin C (1997) Appropriateness of acute medical admissions and length of stay. *Journal of the Royal College of Physicians of London* **31**: 527–532.
- Smith M, Rousseau N, Gregson B, Bond J and Rodgers H (1997) Are older people satisfied with discharge information? *Nursing Times* **93**: 52–53.
- South J (1999) Eligibility criteria and entitlements: defining need for NHS continuing care. *Social Policy and Administration* **33**: 132–149.
- Stevens R (1970) Reasons for admitting patients to geriatric hospitals. *Gerontologica Clinica* **12**: 219–228.
- Sutcliffe P (1991) Government policy in action: good discharge of patients leaving general hospitals. *British Journal of Occupational Therapy* **54**: 57–60.
- Tierney AJ (ed.) (1993) *Discharge of Patients from Hospital*. Nursing Research Unit, Department of Nursing Studies, University of Edinburgh.
- Tierney A and Closs SJ (1993) Discharge planning for elderly patients. *Nursing Standard* **7**: 30–33.
- Tierney AJ and Worth A (1995) Review: readmission of elderly patients to hospital. *Age and Ageing* **24**: 163–166.

- Torrance N, Lawson H, Hogg B and Knox J (1972) Acute admissions to medical beds. *Journal of the Royal College of General Practitioners* **22**: 211–219.
- Tsang P and Severs M (1995) A study of appropriateness of acute geriatric admissions and an assessment of the Appropriateness Evaluation Protocol. *Journal of the Royal College of Physicians of London* **29**: 311–314.
- Twigg J (1997) Deconstructing the 'social bath': help with bathing at home for older and disabled people. *Journal of Social Policy* **26**: 211–232.
- Victor C (1992) From pillow to post. *Health Service Journal*, 13 August, 20–22.
- Victor C and Khakoo A (1994) Is hospital the right place? A survey of 'inappropriate' admissions to an inner London NHS Trust. *Journal of Public Health Medicine* **16**: 286–290.
- Victor C and Vetter NJ (1985) The early readmission of the elderly to hospital. *Age and Ageing* **14**: 37–42.
- Vincent J (1995) *Inequality and Old Age*. London, UCL Press.
- Walker A (1980) The social creation of poverty and dependence in old age. *Journal of Social Policy* **9**: 49–75.
- Waters K (1987) Outcomes of discharge from hospital for elderly people. *Journal of Advanced Nursing* **12**: 347–355.
- Wheeler R (1986) Housing policy and elderly people. In: C Phillipson and A Walker (eds) *Ageing and Social Policy: a critical assessment*. Aldershot, Gower.
- White C (1999) A united front. *Community Care*, 3 June, 30–31.
- Wistow G and Fuller S (1982) *Joint Planning in Perspective*. Birmingham, Centre for Research in Social Policy and National Association of Health Authorities.
- Worth A, Tierney AJ and Lockerbie L (1994) Community nurses and discharge planning. *Nursing Standard* **8**: 25–30.
- Worth A, Tierney AJ and Watson NT (2000) Discharged from hospital: should more responsibility for meeting patients' and carers' information needs now be shouldered in the community? *Health and Social Care in the Community* **8**: 398–405.

Index